# The 3 Rs of E-Mail
## Risks, Rights and Responsibilities

by
Diane B. Hartman
and
Karen S. Nantz

# The 3 Rs of E-Mail
## Risks, Rights, and Responsibilities

Diane B. Hartman and Karen Nantz

**Credits**
Managing Editor: *Kathleen Barcos*
Editor: *Kay Keppler*
Designer: *ExecuStaff*
Typesetter: *ExecuStaff*
Cover Design: *London Road Design*

Copyright © 1996 by Crisp Publications, Inc.

Printed in the United States of America by Bawden Printing Company.

**Library of Congress Catalog Card Number 95-74725**
Hartman, Diane and Nantz, Karen
The 3 Rs of E-Mail
ISBN 1-56052-378-6

# Contents

 **Preface**

Many books and articles have been published recently to keep pace with the increased interest in and use of electronic messaging. Most of these books and articles, however, focus on the technology rather than on the human effects. In contrast, this awareness-building book attempts to identify and clarify some of the key human issues. Because some of these issues may have serious legal implications that are subject to varying interpretations based on jurisdiction and circumstances, we approach these issues generally to avoid misleading our readers.

The authors and publisher have used their best efforts in preparing this book, but we cannot guarantee any interpretation, instructions and suggestions it contains. This book is not legal advice. All legal decisions related to e-mail should be reviewed by competent legal counsel.

# About This Book

Finding a single source to address the risks, rights and responsibilities of e-mail communication has been a problem up until now. *The 3 Rs of E-mail* is the only book that provides you with up-to-date information and application exercises about the things people fear most about using e-mail: loss of privacy, security, legal implications, appropriate use, effective communication and etiquette.

Whether using e-mail to send a quick business note or to access the Internet with its thousands of networks, you'll benefit from reading this book, completing the exercises and then using the book as a reference for future e-mail issues. You can approach this book in several ways, including:

♦ **Individual, Self-paced Study.** Move as fast or as slow as you like through each section. Start with the self-assessment at the beginning of each section to test your knowledge of the issues. Then study the key points, apply the concepts to real-life examples and reflect on how these concepts fit your unique situation.

♦ **Workshops and Seminars.** This book provides the basics for understanding and using e-mail effectively in any situation. As a workbook for a seminar or tutorial, this book sets the foundation for an e-mail learning environment. Use the self-assessments as both pre- and posttests. Go beyond theory to focused application by completing the exercises. Use the checklists and resource guides to foster continuous learning.

♦ **Distance Learning.** Use this book for self-paced learning for those who cannot attend "home office" training. The easy-to-read format guarantees everyone from technical to nontechnical readers will benefit.

# About the Authors

**Diane B. Hartman** is a partner in Advanced Communication Solutions (ADCOMS) and an international communications consultant. She has a masters degree in business education and administrative management from Brigham Young University and has taught business and communication skills at every level. Ms. Hartman has more than 25 years' business experience, is a course developer and trainer and coauthor of two editions of *Effective Writing: A Practical Grammar Review.* She also has written award-winning articles for national magazines. Her e-mail address is DHadcoms@aol.com.

**Karen S. Nantz, Ph.D.,** is an associate professor in the Lumpkin College of Business and Applied Sciences at Eastern Illinois University. Dr. Nantz has 15 years' teaching experience and extensive business and computer consulting experience. She has written about computer use, electronic mail and curriculum development and is a frequent presenter at information systems conferences. She is an active member of the Information Resources Management Association, the International Business Schools Computer Users Group, the International Association for Computer Information Systems and the Office Systems Research Association. Her e-mail address is cfksn@eiu.edu.

 **Introduction**

The forerunners of electronic mail (e-mail) have been around for more than 100 years. Samuel Morse's telegraph was developed in the 1830s and Alexander Bain's first facsimile machine (the "recording telegraph") not much later. E-mail as we know it today was developed by the federal government in the 1960s and used extensively as a research tool and information exchange mechanism only by federal employees and university researchers until the 1980s, when the technology was released and commercial applications entered the business world. Many businesspeople found electronic mail to be faster, more versatile, more convenient and more spontaneous than traditional methods of communication. For example, compare the typical manual steps in Figure 1 that a manager might use to create a message with the electronic steps in Figure 2.

**Figure 1: Manual Steps for Creating Messages**

Manager wants to send message

Manager writes key ideas

Manager dictates message

Secretary transcribes and types message

Manager reviews and edits draft

Secretary finalizes message

Manager signs message

Secretary mails or hand distributes message

## Figure 2: Electronic Steps for Creating Messages

Manager wants to send message

Manager uses computer to create message

Manager e-mails message

Eight steps have been reduced to three; what might have taken an hour or even a day to accomplish is now completed probably in less than 10 minutes and instantaneously distributed to anyone worldwide.

E-mail economics makes sense, too. Let's say you need to get a paper document from California to New York overnight. Figure 3 shows a comparison of four ways to get the documentation from coast to coast overnight. The savings might be even more dramatic if you sent the document to a distant point on the globe.[1]

## Figure 3: E -Mail Economics

| | |
|---|---|
| $13.00 | Letter sent overnight via common carrier |
| 4.56 | Letter sent telex/telegram |
| 1.86 | Fax |
| .16 | Electronic mail |

Today, e-mail is an established part of business communications. Its rapid growth is credited not only to computer technology and the availability of personal computers and other sophisticated communicating devices, but also to promises of increased speed, efficiency and effectiveness.

Besides being available on every type of computer system, e-mail fuels the Internet, the world's largest computer network and commonly called the "Information Highway." Every public and private e-mail system can have a gateway to the Internet.

Even though e-mail holds many promises, few users understand the full ramifications of its use. Among the concerns of e-mail users are a loss of privacy, information overload, a demand for new skills and a loss of face-to-face contact.

The purpose of this book is to address these concerns and help you become an informed e-mail user, administrator or owner of an e-mail system. When you finish this book, you'll understand your e-mail risks, rights and responsibilities, so that you can reap the rewards promised by the technology. Whether you use e-mail for business or personal use, you'll find answers to perplexing questions that will help you maximize e-mail benefits as you lessen e-mail drawbacks. What's more, you'll be able to communicate clearly and legally without offending others.

# Dedication

**Diane B. Hartman:** Thank you to the family and friends who never lost faith in our ability to write this book and who gave support and encouragement along the way. Many thanks to those we surveyed, company management and end users, and to those online users who provided insights into the electronic community.

**Karen S. Nantz:** This book would not have been possible without the love and support of family and friends. I would especially like to thank my husband, and my good friends, Mary and Joe Hillock. I would also like to thank all of the e-mail users who have opened their e-mail files to us. This book is for you.

A special thanks to our advisory board who shared their e-mail expertise, offered suggestions, reviewed our material and encouraged us:

Dr. James S. O'Rourke IV
Professor, Business Communication
Notre Dame University

Robert Mirguet
Systems administrator

Jeff Ubois
Contributing editor
*Digital Media*
*Internet World*
*Midrange Systems*

Jonathan Rosenoer, Software creator
CyberLaw and CyberLex

James Barresi, Attorney
Employment Law

 # An E-Mail Primer

According to the Electronic Messaging Association, electronic mail (e-mail) is the generic name for noninteractive communication of text, data, image or voice messages between a sender and recipients by systems using telecommunications links. What does that mean for you and me? It means that we can use a computer that is electronically linked to another computer to communicate.

We can use e-mail to create, send, receive, forward, reply, edit or delete messages sent from one computer to another. Each e-mail user has an electronic storage space called a mailbox. You can receive mail at the electronic mailbox just as you receive mail at a post office box, only instead of a key for your mailbox, you have a password. Each e-mail system has a postmaster (called a system administrator) who controls the resources. Just as the postmaster of the post office can access your post office box, a system administrator can access your electronic mailbox.

E-mail is so versatile that it can take the place of phone calls, facsimile (fax) messages and written messages, such as memos and reports. It gives you the opportunity to send a message to someone across the hall or around the world.

The following common electronic messaging terms will be used throughout the book. Other terms may be found in the glossary.

### Common Terms

*Local Area Network (LAN)*  A computer network that links computers together at a single site, such as a department or building. Local area networks allow users to share hardware, software and data and to send and receive data and graphics files.

*Wide Area Network (WAN)*  A computer network that links computers together in a wide geographical area. A WAN functions the same as a LAN, but allows wide distribution of data and graphics files.

*Internet*

A system of wide area networks supported by universities, research centers and government agencies that allows international transmission of data.

*Newsgroup*

A newsgroup is a place within a LAN or WAN where discussions on a particular topic take place. Users can send and receive articles from the newsgroup.

*Mail Address*

A mail address is the unique electronic location of your e-mail files. A mail address usually consists of two parts: the name of the host computer where your e-mail system is located and your specific mailing address. For example: jsmith@abccorp.com might be the mailing address for John Smith at ABC Corporation.

*Flaming*

A flame or flaming is an attack on another user or group of users. A flame contains derogatory or embarrassing information that may include insensitive, profane or obscene language.

# Nature of E-Mail

*"There is nothing more difficult to take in hand,*
*more perilous to conduct, or more uncertain in its success,*
*than to take the lead in the introduction of a new order of things."*

—Niccolo Machiavelli
*The Prince* (1532)

Many people do not understand the nature of e-mail or how e-mail can work for them. Take this self-assessment quiz to check what you know.

─── S e l f - A s s e s s m e n t ───

How well do you understand the nature of e-mail? Check "yes" if the statement is true for you; check "no" if it is not. By completing the self-assessment before reading this section, you will identify strengths and weaknesses and focus your study efforts. When you complete the assessment, compare your answers with the key at the end of the quiz.

|  | Yes | No |
|---|---|---|
| 1. Most of e-mail's problems stem from hardware and software deficiencies. | ☐ | ☐ |
| 2. Most people receive adequate e-mail training, including how to manage e-mail effectively. | ☐ | ☐ |
| 3. E-mail productivity is rapidly increasing. | ☐ | ☐ |
| 4. A message sent electronically is equivalent to dropping a letter in a U.S. mailbox and therefore cannot be recalled. | ☐ | ☐ |
| 5. Filters or previewing are the two most effective ways to reduce unwanted e-mail. | ☐ | ☐ |

Key: 1. N, 2. N, 3. N, 4. N, 5. Y

Flexible and powerful electronic mail is taking the country and the world by storm and is projected to continue its dramatic increase. In fact, twice the number of users will send four times as much mail as intercompany messaging grows.[1] A survey by Xerox and Cognitive Communications of employee communication experts at *Fortune* 100 corporations reveals that 9 out of 10 corporations use e-mail for person-to-person communication, and two-thirds use e-mail to disseminate publications.[2]

E-mail attracts both organizations and individuals through its promise of speedy messages worldwide, connections to databases of information and live chat sessions with the famous and ordinary. More than 6.3 million people subscribe to online services, and the number continues to grow.[3] America Online's president Steve Case reported that in May 1995, America Online (AOL) passed the three million member milestone—making AOL the largest commercial online service.[4]

So great is the response to e-mail that the U.S. Post Office attributed its reported 6% decline in business-to-business first class mail for 1994 to e-mail and fax machines.[5]

Obviously, millions of people are anxious to reap the rewards of using e-mail. However, lurking in the shadows are some demanding challenges that could threaten this technology's potential. Jeremy Rifkin's *The End of Work* warns that the new information technology poses a threat of mass unemployment and social unrest.[6] Clifford Stoll in *Silicon Snake Oil* says that e-mail is "often undependable and annoying to access; it's usually impersonal and boring. A handwritten letter is arguably cheaper, more reliable, and far more expressive. In some instances, it can even be faster." He differs from those who think e-mail and networks will bolster our productivity and foster a paperless office.[7]

Our own research has shown that organizations are hesitant about connecting, especially to the Internet. Other studies, such as *Beyond Computing's* January/February fax poll, acknowledges this hesitancy in its June 1995 issue. Many companies hold back because they question the benefits gained for the dollars spent; they are concerned about security issues and the time and effort needed to use the Internet effectively.[8]

# Benefits and Drawbacks

Still, the craving for instantaneous connections, wide distribution and reduced phone and meeting time stimulates e-mail use. What benefits and drawbacks have you experienced with e-mail? If you are new to e-mail or anticipate using it, which ones have you heard about? Check all that apply in the following lists:

| Benefits | Drawbacks |
|---|---|
| ☐ Improved productivity | ☐ No response |
| ☐ Communication speed | ☐ Reduced productivity |
| ☐ Wide distribution | ☐ Slow response |
| ☐ Flexibility | ☐ Increased message load |
| ☐ Document sharing | ☐ Increased tension |
| ☐ Databases | ☐ Weakened morale |
| ☐ Computer forums | ☐ User resistance |
| ☐ Empowerment | ☐ Lack of feedback |

| Benefits *(continued)* | Drawbacks *(continued)* |
|---|---|
| ☐ Paper reduction | ☐ Distrust |
| ☐ Simultaneous distribution | ☐ Increased errors |
| ☐ Time/cost savings | ☐ Poorly written messages |
| ☐ Less phone tag | ☐ Misdirected messages |
| ☐ Reduced time/distance barriers | ☐ Invaded privacy |
| ☐ Shortened cycle for written communications | ☐ Poor/no reader feedback |
| ☐ Improved morale | ☐ Lost messages |
| ☐ Employee loyalty | ☐ Poor security |
| ☐ Prompt messages | ☐ Guarded information |
| ☐ Improved customer relations | ☐ Reduced interaction |
| ☐ Flattened organizational hierarchy | ☐ Mistakes publicized |
| ☐ Creativity stimulated | ☐ Added structure |
| ☐ Resolved problems | ☐ Incessant talk |
| ☐ Personal messages | ☐ Rudeness or discourtesy |
| | ☐ Inappropriate messages |
| | ☐ Flaming |
| | ☐ Sexual harassment |
| | ☐ Copyright/license infringement |
| | ☐ Increased transmission/storage costs |

The number of benefits and drawbacks that you checked is not as important as your understanding the common thread that binds each category. What do all the benefits have in common? What do all of the drawbacks have in common? The benefits are mostly associated with the technology, whereas the drawbacks are mostly associated with the way people use the technology.

Mentioning some of e-mail's less publicized, but none the less spectacular, benefits seems appropriate here. Included are enjoying companionship, reaching out to family and friends and providing life-saving efforts for the elderly.

A Boston woman slowed by Parkinson's Disease was rescued from a medical emergency because her SeniorNet chat partners alerted police. ("Computer net turns into safety net for ailing online senior citizen" *Charleston Times Courier*, Charleston, Illinois, January 24, 1995, C4.)

**The 3 R's of E-Mail**

A computer specialist who suffered a heart attack at his desk tapped out an e-mail SOS that saved his life. "For me, e-mail means emergency mail," the New York senior said. (Associated Press, "E-mail SOS brings dozens to the rescue," *Deseret News*, Salt Lake City, Utah, April 1, 1994.)

When Josh Knauer, a senior at Carnegie Mellon University, wants to communicate with relatives, telephoning is his last choice. He prefers to tap out a message on his computer keyboard. "It definitely saves money on long distance." And he's not the only family member hooked on e-mail. His parents use e-mail to communicate with all three of their children living in different areas of the country. (Karla Price, "On Campus, there's a letter in the e-mail," *USA Today*, Wednesday, October 5, 1994, p6D.)

IDT has developed an audio Internet mail service for blind and dyslexic people or for those adverse to learning computer skills. Under this system, you have an Internet e-mail address. When you receive a message, the system calls you and a voice synthesizer reads the message over the phone. The voice message can also be routed to a voice-mail system for delayed retrieval. Its only drawback is that you cannot send or reply to messages. (*The Seybold Report on Desktop Publishing*, June 6, 1994, v8 n10, p43.)

## Common Factor Behind Drawbacks

More is written about e-mail's benefits than its drawbacks. What is written about drawbacks tends to emphasize the human effects. Part of the reason for these drawbacks is that few people receive adequate training. We're not speaking about equipment and software training, although some receive little of that, either. What we are referring to is reflected in our 1994 national end-user study.

Respondents indicated that most users receive training on hardware and software use, but few organizations place emphasis on communication skills, records management, appropriate use and etiquette. Just think of what technology's potential might be if human management of e-mail could improve at the same exponential rate as the technology. Such a thought boggles the mind.

## Leading Drawback

E-mail's leading drawback is reduced productivity. Even though e-mail promises instant connections and access to previously inaccessible resources, it often delivers a blitz of trivia. The amount has become so overwhelming that Charles Wang, chairman of Computer Associates International Inc., no longer sends or reads e-mail—even though his organization sells an e-mail software package. Wang even shuts down the organization's e-mail system for five hours a day to encourage worker productivity.[9]

Part of the problem is the ease with which people can deliberately or accidentally bombard electronic mailboxes. Once sent, messages may be difficult, if not impossible to recall. Consider the person who, intending to send a confidential letter to one person, accidentally sends it to 100 people. Some companies of e-mail systems equate an e-mail letter to dropping a letter in a mailbox: It can't be recalled. However, some e-mail systems can recall mail, even if one of the intended recipients has already read it.

Not being able to recall sent mail does not explain the overload problem. Poor e-mail management is a big part of the problem. People dump volumes of unnecessary information into the e-mail system. In one study surveying 96 workers ranging from secretaries to managers with an average of five years' e-mail experience, employees sent two messages a day and received 26. Of messages received, 21 were addressed to groups rather than individuals; only three out of five were related to the organization's work. This mixture of personal and business e-mail translates into an average of 38 nonwork uses per person per week compared to only 6 times a week for the phone.[10]

Message overload is not restricted just to the in-house system. Consider this fictitious scenario about Jim Smith, who uses his e-mail system to access the

Internet. Jim logs into the newsgroup *rec.books.mystery.sherlock.holmes,* a group interested in mysteries written by Sir Arthur Conan Doyle. Jim uses his organization's computer resources to tell his group that one of the cable channels is showing a Holmes movie tonight.

The newsgroup Jim accesses is a mail list—that is, every message sent to this newsgroup goes to one location and then is distributed to everyone who subscribes to the newsgroup. Let's say that 1,000 users subscribe. The average number of messages each user receives daily is 50. That's 50,000 messages sent across the Internet just from this one newsgroup.

How much does it cost to send a message? One list administrator estimates that each message costs $.05. For Jim's single message to reach all 1,000 users—$50. All the traffic for just one day (1,000 subscribers × 50 messages per day) is $2,500. Jim isn't paying for it, so who is? The computer site that houses the newsgroup files has to pay to be connected to the Internet. It also has to pay to connect to the Internet. It has storage and maintenance costs, and it is paying the salary of whoever administers the newsgroup.

Do you think Jim is an exception to e-mail users in most organizations? Probably not. Almost half (39.9%) of the people we surveyed used e-mail for both business and personal use. Think about the messages you have sent this week. How many were necessary? How many were business messages? How many were personal? Do you contribute to the overload?

Add the cost of message overload to monies already spent to maintain personal computers in the organization's system, and you have a major financial concern. Some companies may already spend as much as $3,830 annually to maintain just one computer. Although these costs are expected to drop by 50% over a three-year period as standards and technologies improve, hidden costs such as message overload and reduced productivity can and will offset gains.[11]

## Answers to Overload

To counter excessive e-mail use, some users have suggested charging for e-mail messages, much the same as if you were sending a letter. Billing users, however, would be an electronic nightmare.

People are bombarded with unwanted e-mail. How are they managing the deluge? Some use a "filter," a utility program that allows the user to screen incoming messages. User's tell the mail server their preferences and the software forwards only those messages. For example, in one system, you can tell the software to skip any messages that exceed a certain size, or you can tell it to reject messages from particular senders. You can even disgard messages.

Previewing is another option. When previewing, users can look at mail headers to determine which messages to read (Figure 1). For now, most e-mail systems offer either filters or previewing, but not a combination.

**Figure 1: Message Header**

| | |
|---|---|
| TO: | athomas |
| FR: | bdaines |
| DATE: | June 10, 199X |
| RE: | Team Meeting June 15, 199X—Reply by June 13, 199X |

Another safeguard is to appoint one person as the mail list gatekeeper who does all the e-mail posting. Another is to send a list of etiquette rules warning that those who break the rules will be flamed. Still another is to threaten sending a 20-million-character file to the senders of unwanted e-mail. For those messages that slip through all defenses, you might send a screenful of "not interested" messages. No one choice seems ideal for everyone.

## Legality Is Another Concern

Some e-mail users find that e-mail messages may be illegal. In several instances, government officials have been told that e-mailing constituents may violate open-meeting laws. For example, last year in Texas, a city council member was forced to retract an e-mail message sent to the home of a colleague. In Palo Alto, California, lawmakers were chastised by the city attorney for discussing an issue by e-mail.

Many government officials easily discard e-mail messages because they do not consider them public record. In addition, many haven't found a way to store messages efficiently. The result is a controversy that discourages many government officials from using the technology. Although they allow their staff to use it, government officials prefer to avoid any appearance of wrongdoing.

# Summary

Electronic mail offers speed, instant information access, companionship, life-saving services and visits with family and friends. E-mail capabilities are changing the way we live and do business.

Still, the technology is not without its problems, and difficult challenges lie ahead. Hardware and software problems are fundamental, legal issues remain to be solved and human use factors such as message overload, reduced productivity and increased costs may stand in the way of widespread acceptance of electronic mail. Individual knowledge of the risks, rights and responsibilities will go a long way to dispel these concerns.

# E-Mail Risks

*❝Life is full of risks, but being ignorant of the risks
is the riskiest of all.❞*

E-mail provides great opportunities to exchange messages with coworkers and others worldwide, but such open communication does involve risk, especially legal risk. Deliberately or unintentionally, "people [can] act and react to the virtual world online without considering the law."[1]

People seem to think this electronic environment is somehow outside the law that applies to other communication media such as the phone, fax or surface mail ("snail mail" to e-mail users). E-mailers upload and download files without questioning if their actions are legal or even ethical. Their actions put them, their e-mail systems and their organizations at risk.

Seven risks should especially concern anyone associated with e-mail.

- ♦ Who owns the e-mail message?
- ♦ When is e-mail private?
- ♦ Who can legally read e-mail messages?
- ♦ What legally can be uploaded and downloaded?
- ♦ How secure are e-mail messages?
- ♦ Are e-mail messages part of an official record?
- ♦ How safely and legally can business be conducted through e-mail?

E-mail messages are transmitted by in-house systems and across public and private networks nationally and internationally. The ease with which messages are transmitted creates an illusion of privacy and unrestricted communication. This illusion is enhanced by the nature of the Internet. No one owns or controls the Internet—yet—and large networks are decentralized both technically and governmentally. No one central hub routes messages.

For e-mail users, sending and receiving electronic messages with their wildly diverse content to a possibly widespread and large audience with the promise of organizing groups and affecting public policy carries the excitement that pamphleteering must have done in prerevolutionary America. So far, judges and legislators have not done much to restrict this electronic "speech," but they will. In 1995 the Senate and the House passed bills that would regulate some areas of electronic communication. A case filed in federal court against one online service was decided in favor of the plaintiff, who argued that he was libeled in a message sent by a former employee, and the libel affected his business. The online service has appealed.

For now, most laws that govern electronic communication are found in state constitutions, federal and state statutes and judicial interpretations. Federal interpretations will evolve as cases work their way through the lower courts, but the main law regulating electronic messaging today is the Electronic Communications Privacy Act (ECPA), amended in 1986 to include digital electronic communication. (See more about the ECPA in the "Rights" section.) At this time, it is clearly the most important statute affecting electronic messaging. Basically, the ECPA protects all electronic messaging systems against outside intruders and protects message privacy sent over public lines. Until it is replaced by more stringent laws for electronic technology, it needs to be studied and understood by government agents and businesses and individuals who send e-mail messages over public lines.

Although the ECPA protects both internal and external systems from intruders, it generally does not offer other protections to **internal** systems. Consequently, organizations with solely internal e-mail systems are left to themselves to create effective, secure and enforceable policies and procedures.

With so little to guide public and private entities, and until pending cases are decided or legislation is enacted, appropriately and legally using e-mail rests with organizations, their system administrators and individual users. All must consider the risks, the rights and the responsibilities of electronic messaging to reap its rewards.

# Risk #1: Who Owns the E-mail Message?

—— S e l f - A s s e s s m e n t ——

How well do you understand the risks of e-mail message ownership? Check "yes" if the statement is true for you; check "no" if it is not. By completing the self-assessment before reading this section, you will identify strengths and weaknesses and focus your study efforts. When you complete the assessment, compare your answers with the key at the end of the quiz.

|   | Yes | No |
|---|---|---|
| 1. E-mail ownership and privacy are basically the same issues. | ☐ | ☐ |
| 2. By signing a user agreement or contract, the user automatically waives ownership rights. | ☐ | ☐ |
| 3. Intellectual property laws, such as copyrights, include *all* electronic technology such as e-mail. | ☐ | ☐ |
| 4. The moment an e-mail message becomes fixed in a tangible medium, it is copyrighted—even without a copyright notice. | ☐ | ☐ |
| 5. If an organization claims e-mail message ownership, it has the right to copy and distribute employee messages to external networks. | ☐ | ☐ |
| 6. Most e-mail activities are conducted legally with permission from copyright owners through an implied license. | ☐ | ☐ |

> **Key:** 1. N, 2. N, 3. Y, 4. Y, 5. N, 6. Y

Sally enjoyed using her organization's in-house e-mail system, especially to send messages to friends in other departments. Oftentimes in her messages, she let off steam about work experiences and coworkers. Sometimes she criticized company policies and procedures. Once she vented her frustrations about a customer, describing him in a litany of colorful language. Her use of e-mail as a psychological release abruptly ended one day when her boss called her into his office and confronted her with copies of her e-mail messages. Surprised and angry because she thought her e-mail messages were as private as a personal telephone call, she demanded the copies and threatened to sue. The organization responded with terminating her employment. She, in turn, filed suit for wrongful termination, claiming that employees of the organization had illegally read her e-mail messages and invaded her privacy.

Sound unfair? Unreasonable? Illegal? Not according to a court that awarded judgment to an organization defendant in a similar case. Although Sally's case is hypothetical, the details are similar to the case of *Bourke v. Nissan Motors Corp.* (No. B068705 [Cal.App. 2d Dist., Div. 5, 1993])*. In this case, an

---

*NOTE: Cases cited as legal precedent may not be upheld in other jurisdictions; however, they may have an important influence in similar cases.

employee was fired for sending personal messages through the in-house e-mail system, including some with sexual references. The court ruled against the defendant. Why?

We'll look at the issue of privacy later in this section, but for now, let's focus on who owns Sally's messages, because ownership and privacy are really two separate issues. According to existing copyright law, Sally owns her messages. The minute the messages became fixed in any medium (the organization's e-mail system), they were copyrighted under federal law—even without a copyright notice or registration. Why then did she lose in court?

Sally's privacy rights, not her ownership rights, were in question. Sally and the employee in *Bourke v. Nissan Motors* had both signed a user's agreement limiting their privacy rights. (See Figure 1 for an example of a user's agreement.)

Although each consented to limit individual privacy rights, each did not give up ownership rights. The organization could not copy or distribute Sally's messages outside its e-mail system. In addition, Sally retained these ownership rights.

- ◆ To make modified versions of the messages
- ◆ To distribute the messages
- ◆ To transmit the messages
- ◆ To make the messages public

Is Sally's case limited to the organization's in-house e-mail system? Can you experience this problem on external e-mail systems or on the Internet? Once information leaves the source, what happens to ownership rights? Intellectual property laws, such as copyrights, include *all* electronic technology such as e-mail—whether the system is private or public.

Most e-mail activities are conducted legally with permission from copyright owners through an implied license. Basically, when you send e-mail messages, you implicitly agree that information you make available can be treated like others' information. But the implied license does have limits: you still retain rights not granted in the implied license. Many forget this fact. Some users, for example, think nothing of reposting another person's e-mail messages without permission. Others attach entire articles or files to e-mail messages without permission.

Figure 1: E-Mail User Agreement

# E-MAIL USER AGREEMENT

This e-mail user agreement is a supplement to any and all other employee agreements or policies and reflects my understanding of the conditions under which I may use electronic communication systems. Specifically, I understand and agree to abide by the following provisions of this agreement, knowing that failure to do so may result in an appropriate reprimand or even termination.

1. All electronic communication systems and information transmitted by, received from, and stored in these systems is owned or under the custody of the Company. Since this information has value to the Company, I agree to protect it against unauthorized or unintended use, disclosure, modification, destruction, and interruption or down-grading of availability for continuing operations.

2. I understand that these systems must be used for only job-related purposes as authorized by management and not for personal purposes. Any unauthorized use is a misappropriation. I also understand that I have no expectation of privacy in using this equipment when transmitting, receiving, or storing information.

3. I further understand that the Company may monitor the system at any time at its discretion. Monitoring may include printing and reading electronic messages entering, leaving, or being stored in these systems.

4. I understand that use of an assigned microcomputer or computer terminal is restricted to me and that I should take care to keep that equipment safeguarded from unauthorized use. If an assigned computer is shared, I agree to keep all sensitive information either in regard to confidentiality or privacy on floppy disks or other media that is removable from the computer, and not on an internal hard drive or other media that is usually online and directly accessible in the normal course of computer use.

_____

Name of Employee (Please print)

_____     _____

Employee's Signature                                                          Date

_____

Name of Management Witness (Please print)

_____     _____

Signature of Witness                                                          Date

(Hypothetical example created from ideas expressed in the following sources: Robert J. Nobile, *Guide to Employee Handbooks*, New York: Warren Gorham Lamont, 1994, pp. 9–53; *Guidelines for Company Policies of Employee Privacy in the Electronic Workplace*, Center for Information Technology and Law, College of Business Administration and College of Law, University of Cincinnati, Cincinnati, OH, 1995.)

Several authorities argue that e-mail messages written on the organization's system during work time fall under the "work-for-hire" definition. If so, they are the property of the employer. All copyrighted material produced as part of your employment may be included within this definition: computer files, reports, letters, memos, etc.

Many employers feel that because they purchase the equipment, train the users and pay the communication costs, they have a right and responsibility to make sure the e-mail system is used for business purposes only. In addition, employers fear the consequences of illegal or inappropriate use. For example, claims of e-mail sexual harassment are on the increase. What might seem like a harmless date invitation from an e-mail sender might be construed as sexual harassment by an e-mail receiver. The result could be a lawsuit naming not only the sender but also the organization. Moreover, leaving false messages, downloading pornography and sending racially hostile material are fueling employer concerns.

As in Sally's case, if an organization wants to own e-mail messages, it can ask employees to sign a user contract or agreement granting ownership rights to the organization. Organizations claiming message ownership, however, sometimes find this action irritates workers and creates suspicions about how the organization will use the messages. To avoid such problems, some organizations request that users license the organization to use messages for specific purposes. One purpose might be to collect viewpoints or to excerpt information for group decision making.

# Risk #2: When is E-Mail Private?

## —— S e l f - A s s e s s m e n t ——

How well do you understand the risks of e-mail message privacy? Check "yes" if the statement is true for you; check "no" if it is not. By completing the self-assessment before reading this section, you will identify strengths and weaknesses and focus your study efforts. When you complete the assessment, compare your answers with the key at the end of the quiz.

|  | Yes | No |
|---|---|---|
| 1. The ECPA governs privacy rights of both public and private e-mail systems. | ☐ | ☐ |

2. System administrators are not restricted by the ECPA from disclosing internal employee e-mail messages. ☐ ☐

3. Under most circumstances, legal authorities can review e-mail messages without a warrant. ☐ ☐

4. Deleting an e-mail message from a mailbox guarantees message privacy. ☐ ☐

5. A hybrid organization that provides both internal and public messaging could be subject to ECPA regulations. ☐ ☐

Key: 1. N, 2. Y, 3. N, 4. N, 5. Y

"The laws currently governing commercial transactions, data privacy and intellectual property were largely developed for a time when telegraphs, typewriters and mimeographs were the commonly used office technologies and business was conducted by paper documents sent by mail. Technologies and business practices have dramatically changed, but the law has been slower to adapt." (Information Security and Privacy in Network Environments, Office of Technology Assessment, Joan Winston, Project Director, September 23, 1994).

The question of ownership and privacy rights cross in scope and impact. The only federal law governing electronic communications is the Electronic Communications Privacy Act (ECPA). Under its provisions, *all* e-mail systems are protected from unauthorized outsiders who break into the system, steal or manipulate information or damage the system.

As to its privacy provisions, the ECPA is generally applicable only to an electronic messaging system providing public service. Usually, providers of an internal system need be concerned only with ECPA provisions governing outside intruders and electronic wiretappers. Under the ECPA, e-mail owners of internal systems or their designated employees are not restricted from disclosing messages, including those sent by employees. However, be aware that court cases have already surfaced challenging the right of supervisors, coworkers and systems administrators to read e-mail messages. Although unsuccessful so far, legal experts expect such cases to appear regularly until new legislation specifically addresses the issue.

What about organizations that allow outside users to access their internal systems? For example, say your organization allows its vendors to access the e-mail system to process orders and invoices. In this case, these messages may be disclosed because your organization would be considered the recipient, and the vendor, the sender. The ECPA permits messages sent over public lines to be disclosed if either the sender or receiver gives permission. If, however, the supplier uses the internal system to send a message directly to another outsider, ECPA public restrictions could apply. Interpretation suggests, however, that as long as direct message traffic is limited and outsiders are not charged for messaging, ECPA privacy rules would not apply. Should a company open more of its system to outsiders, ECPA rules might well apply.[2]

A hybrid organization provides both internal and public messaging and is in a legal grey area under the ECPA. If your organization maintains a hybrid e-mail system, be cautious in disclosing messages sent through your system. Otherwise, you and your organization could be exposed to criminal and civil actions.

Even if ECPA restrictions apply to your organization's e-mail system, notable exceptions permit interception or disclosure of messages. These exceptions include interception or disclosure necessary "in the normal course of business, when engaged in activities necessary to providing services, or to protect the rights or property of an electronic mail provider." (18 U.S.C.A. sec. 2511(2)(a)(1) (West Supp. 1988). E-mail service providers may also disclose message contents to law enforcement officials "when the contents were obtained inadvertently and appear to concern the commission of a crime." (18 U.S.C.A. sec. 2511(3)(b)(iv) (West Supp. 1988).

Should a system administrator accidentally review a questionable message, he or she may request that legal authorities review the message. Under most circumstances, legal authorities are not allowed to review messages on their own without a warrant.

Applying the ECPA in our hypothetical case, Sally's company maintained only an internal e-mail system and was not subject to ECPA privacy restrictions. In addition, Sally forgot that as a condition of employment, she signed a user contract or system use agreement. By doing so, she waived her rights under the ECPA. This practice is not uncommon. Some system administrators post a notice that the system should not be considered private for the purposes of the ECPA.

Some of the messages Sally's boss showed her had been sent months ago and deleted from her mailbox. What she didn't realize is that deleting messages from her mailbox did not guarantee they wouldn't surface somewhere else. Messages are often stored on servers and daily, weekly or monthly backup tapes. Deleted messages or those that have been recorded over may be recovered. Even data stored on fire-damaged equipment can sometimes be recovered.

E-mail can be subpoenaed and used as court evidence. As attorney John Bicket says, "If juries can't see the evidence, they won't remember it. But e-mail is demonstrative proof."[3] Electronic detectives can comb through computer systems and discarded computer files looking for evidence.

An attorney may not even need a subpoena to obtain e-mail messages. Say, for example, an employee sues a company saying she has been sexually harassed in an e-mail message. Once the lawsuit begins, the company defendant can be forced to produce e-mail or answer questions without a subpoena, but the information must be relevant and likely to lead to admissible evidence. Although the defendant company might claim such information is burdensome to produce, the court usually will rule in favor of the plaintiff. (Interview with James Barresi, Employment Law Attorney, Cincinnati, Ohio, June 20, 1995.)

Notable figures have already fallen victim to enduring e-mail. Among them is Oliver North, whose testimony in the Iran-contra affair was challenged after e-mail messages were discovered. In the Rodney King beating trial, Los Angeles police officer Lawrence Powell was confronted with an e-mail message he wrote shortly after the incident: "Oops, I haven't beaten anyone so bad in a long time."[4]

The ECPA allows an internal e-mail system provider and its e-mail users to decide to eliminate privacy or to allow for low, medium or high privacy—even from the system administrator but not from legal authorities. Before deciding, however, all sides should consider the costs involved to guarantee the decided level of privacy and to minimize the threat of government seizure. A strong correlation exists between privacy rights of the system and privacy rights of its users.

If you are an e-mail user who feels defensive about privacy rights and views the organization and its system administrator as the "enemy" infringing on your rights, consider the organization's viewpoint. Management may consider the organization's e-mail system to be primarily an information distribution system. As a distributor, the company may see similarities between itself and other distributors of information—bookstores, libraries, post office or common carriers such as telephone and cable companies. Normally, distributors do not control content. Rather, they provide storage space and mailboxes for information exchange.

If, however, the organization becomes accountable for what flows through the system, its exposure to risk may encourage control. Control might mean requiring the system administrator to check every file and message for inappropriate or illegal use, to limit user access, reduce message volume and limit existing or potential beneficial user services.

Several cases have tested the extent of an organization's responsibility and consequently the need to exercise more control. (For details about these and other cases, see the litigation discussion in the "Rights" section.) In *Cubby, Inc. v. CompuServe, Inc.* (776 F. Supp. 135 [S.D.N.Y. 1991]) a federal court dismissed a defamation suit because CompuServe was viewed as a distributor that did not exercise editorial control over a questionable newsletter. Yet in *Stratton Oakmont, Inc., et al. v. Prodigy Services Company* (NY Supreme Court No. 31063/94 [May 24, 1995]) the court considered Prodigy a publisher with the same responsibilities as a newspaper. Prodigy has settled the decision and left the judicial decision in question.

Organizations may avoid such legal confrontations and outcomes by gathering input from all affected by e-mail—management, system administrator, human resources, legal counsel and representatives from all user groups. In this way, most risks can be identified and addressed in an e-mail policy that protects not only the organization but also its users from liability risks.

Allowing some e-mail privacy and formally announcing and enforcing that privacy does offer some search and seizure protection to organizations. Government agents generally need a warrant to conduct such searches. Precedent for search and seizure was set in *Steve Jackson v. The U.S. Secret Service* (*Steve Jackson Games, Inc. v. U.S. Secret Service*, 816 F. Supp. 432 [W.D. Texas 1993]) *aff'd; (Steve Jackson Games, Inc. v. U.S. Secret Service*, No. 93-8661 [5th Cir., Oct 31, 1994]). U.S. government agents were seeking a hacker group known as "Legion of Doom" and thought the group could be found at Steve Jackson Games. Agents confiscated the computer equipment and other items key to daily business operations, resulting in serious financial setbacks for the organization.

Besides the ECPA, other federal rulings relate to privacy. Although not e-mail privacy per se, state laws provide some strong arguments for an employee's right to e-mail privacy. Ten states have privacy provisions in their constitutions (Alaska, Arizona, California, Florida, Hawaii, Illinois, Louisiana, Montana, South Carolina, and Washington). More have interpreted their constitutions to create an implied privacy right.[5]

Expectation of privacy can also result from an organization and its system administrator ignoring unrestricted e-mail message use. It can also arise from the practices, policies, and procedures of the organization. The result can be an implied agreement for users to expect e-mail message privacy. Even if the organization and its system administrator take notice and inform users that e-mail messages are no longer private, the notice applies only to future messages and not to ones already transmitted through the system.

If you use a home computer to send e-mail, these messages may be less private than an organization's e-mail messages. Messages sent on smaller, less formal services through the Internet may be stored in numerous host computers before being sent to addressees. Who can guarantee someone won't read your messages along the way? The best solution to privacy threats is to avoid writing anything in an e-mail message you wouldn't want to see on the front page of a newspaper. However, if you must guarantee privacy, encrypt your message before posting.

Don't forget that careless acts also account for invasions of privacy. Are you guilty of leaving your computer unattended? Have you shared your password with others? Have you chosen an obvious password like your name or birth date? Have you been using the same password for several months? These and other actions can threaten your privacy—even when the organization goes to great expense to secure the system.

# Risk #3: Who Can Read E-mail Messages?

## ——— Self-Assessment ———

How well do you understand the risks of monitoring e-mail messages? Check "yes" if the statement is true for you; check "no" if it is not. By completing the self-assessment before reading this section, you will identify strengths and weaknesses and focus your study efforts. When you complete the assessment, compare your answers with the key at the end of the quiz.

|  | Yes | No |
|---|---|---|
| 1. Some companies are required by law to monitor e-mail message activity. | ☐ | ☐ |
| 2. Few legal precedents assist organizations in resolving the monitoring dilemma. | ☐ | ☐ |

**The 3 R's of E-Mail**

3. If organizations do not monitor and their employees send inappropriate or illegal e-mail messages, these organizations and their system administrators might be held liable. ☐ ☐

4. If an employee sends an inappropriate or illegal message unrelated to his or her regular employment duties or during personal time, the organization and its system administrator might be shielded from liability. ☐ ☐

5. Pending e-mail legislation emphasizes more responsibility rather than less for organizations and their system administrators. ☐ ☐

**Key:** 1. Y, 2. Y, 3. Y, 4. Y, 5. Y

Monitoring e-mail is a reviewing task usually delegated to the system administrator. Some believe that monitoring is necessary to reduce the risks of illegal activities. Others think monitoring is a policing duty beyond the scope of the organization and its system administrator. In fact, they think regular monitoring is a waste of valuable time and energy. Nevertheless, many private and public organizations find themselves somewhere between the two extremes—monitoring some messaging areas and not others.

Does your organization monitor your e-mail messages? Does your subscription service monitor messages and real-time chat? Have you received notice you are being monitored? Studies reveal that millions of Americans are monitored by their organizations—knowingly and unknowingly.

Some companies are required by law to monitor e-mail message activity. The Securities and Exchange Commission mandates that publicly traded firms monitor e-mail that is transmitted outside the organization's network. Not doing so may result in an organization being held negligent for failing to protect vital information.[6] Under the ECPA, an e-mail provider may "randomly monitor communications as part of its quality control operations or to mechanically maintain its system, but is not entitled to purposefully monitor the communications of a particular customer." (18 U.S.C.A. sec 2511(2)(a)(i) (West Supp. 1988).

More organizations appear to be sidestepping the monitoring issue or conducting arbitrary snooping that could be labeled harassing or even illegal. Misinterpreted to infringe on others' rights, monitoring activities may encourage mandates from the courts, Congress and trade unions. Little legal precedent helps resolve the monitoring dilemma.

The Electronic Communications Forwarding Act (ECFA), proposed in Congress a few years ago would have relieved system administrators of legal responsibility for users' actions. ECFA never surfaced for a vote, but some think the act may be revived, since e-mail lawsuits questioning legal responsibility are increasing.[7]

If an organization gives employees access to external networks, and an employee sends an e-mail message from the in-house system defaming a competitor, that message would bear the organization's header. As a result, one employee's opinion might be construed as reflecting the organization's opinion. Remember Sally? During her lunch hour, Sally transmitted her flaming messages through the in-house e-mail system. Sally exaggerated her comments about a competitor to the point of telling outright lies. If the recipient of Sally's message passes it along to a friend who gives it to the libeled competitor, the competitor could sue the organization and Sally. (Since Sally sent this and other messages that were unrelated to her regular employment duties during her lunch hour, the organization might be shielded from liability.) However, shielding an organization from liability is not a clear standard. The more power and responsibility an employee has in the company, the more courts may look upon his or her activities—even during the lunch hour—as related to the job.

Probably the best approach to monitoring is to apply common sense and avoid risk to everyone involved. Above all, remember that e-mail messages are not private and are long-lasting.

# Risk #4 What Can Be Legally Uploaded and Downloaded?

—— Self-Assessment ——

How well do you understand risks associated with uploading or downloading files via e-mail? Check "yes" if the statement is true for you; check "no" if it is not. By completing the self-assessment before reading this section, you will identify strengths and weaknesses and focus your study efforts. When you complete the assessment, compare your answers with the key at the end of the quiz.

|  | Yes | No |
|---|---|---|
| 1. Using someone's ideas in an e-mail message is legal, as long as the ideas are expressed in your own words. | ☐ | ☐ |
| 2. Scanning the full text of an article or book and including it in an e-mail message violates the author's rights. | ☐ | ☐ |
| 3. You can usually post an official government document, law or statute or a pamphlet from a federal agency without concern. | ☐ | ☐ |
| 4. To be on the safe side, avoid copying anything without permission. | ☐ | ☐ |
| 5. Most digitized images found on bulletin boards may infringe on someone's rights. | ☐ | ☐ |
| 6. All clip art files are public domain and can be used legally without violating another's rights. | ☐ | ☐ |
| 7. E-mail chatting provided by subscription services is usually not copyrighted. | ☐ | ☐ |
| 8. Saying what you think or feel is a guaranteed right for both the public and private sectors under the First and Fourteenth Amendments. | ☐ | ☐ |
| 9. Text, still images, digitized images, animation and even sound can qualify as offensive sexual material that can put you at risk. | ☐ | ☐ |

Key: 1. Y, 2. Y, 3. Y, 4. Y, 5. Y, 6. N, 7. N, 8. N, 9. Y

What seems to make monitoring necessary is the questionable activities of many e-mail users—for example, Jake. Not having access to the Internet through the organization's e-mail system, Jake invested in a multimedia home computer system and subscribed to an online service offering a gateway to the Internet. As he "surfed" the Net and chatted with people worldwide, he found he could say just about anything he wanted to on any subject—all under the pseudonym

"Rambo." E-mail buddies shared Internet addresses where he could find a wealth of information to download—everything from text files to digitized "adult" pictures. With his new supergraphics package, he downloaded images, altered them and printed them as gifts for his friends. After his initial investment, this new-found online world of information, pictures and sounds was a great bargain for just a few dollars a month.

*Copyrights in Cyberspace.* Jake's "anything-goes" attitude is typical of many in the electronic community, whether accessing private or public e-mail systems. No wonder organizations and their system administrators fear for the safety of their systems.

Perhaps Jake doesn't know what actions are legal or illegal. Many users remain blissfully ignorant of e-mail legal implications. Their zest for the technology's benefits blinds them to obvious and not-so-obvious consequences.

You've learned about your message ownership rights. Without your permission, the general rule is that others cannot distribute, copy, modify, transmit or make public your messages. Yet, because of the loose nature of electronic messaging, many disregard these rights—thinking they don't apply in cyberspace. Here are some areas where questionable activities could put you at risk.

♦ *Using others' e-mail:* Just as others cannot use your e-mail in ways inconsistent with your rights, neither can you use theirs in ways inconsistent with their rights. Say, for example, you send e-mail messages to someone who in return shares an original short story with you. You cannot copy, sell or publicly use that story without obtaining that person's permission. You can, however, make fair use of the story by quoting a few lines or summarizing the content.

Ownership of your e-mail message does not excuse you from liability if you misuse another's content in your message. For example, if you scan in the full text of an article or book and send it with your e-mail message, you have violated the author's rights.

♦ *Reposting messages:* In the guise of sharing information with others, you cannot repost a message to others without the owner's permission. The author may grant this permission absolutely or might allow you to redistribute the message under certain conditions, including redistributing only part of the message or giving credit as specified by the author. An author might specify that a message may be redistributed if it is used only for personal or classroom use.

If you decide to post an official government document, law or statute or a pamphlet from a federal agency, you can probably do so without concern. These documents fall under the public domain category. However, formatting, sequencing, comments and even summaries can be copyrighted. To be on the safe side, avoid copying anything without permission. (More about public domain in the "Rights" section.)

Lately, owners of copyrighted material are aggressively seeking redress against copyright violations—including not only injunctions to stop others from misusing their work but also damages for losses sustained. In addition, criminal charges may be filed in some of the pending cases. (See "Rights" section for details about pending cases.)

♦ *Duplicating and distributing digitized images:* E-mail message senders often attach other text files and even digitized image files. *All* digitized images are considered copyrighted. Consequently, what you find on most bulletin boards could well infringe on someone's rights.[8] A good example of this is *Playboy* magazine's suit against a bulletin board service for providing online copies of photographs from its magazine.

Many owners of images give an implied license to distribute the images. By the same implied license, users may download the images for personal viewing. Users may not, however, further distribute the images.

For those who like to download images, alter them or combine them in some way to produce an original work, do so cautiously. If you copy without permission, you have violated copyright law. Even if you can't detect someone's original work in your own, if that person suspects you have copied his or her original creation, that person can sue for copyright violation.

If you use clip art files, be aware that these files can be copyrighted individually and as collections. In fact, more than one person's copyright might be involved. For example, an individual image within a collection may be copyrighted by the creator of that image; and the entire collection of images may also be copyrighted by the collection's owner.

♦ *Real-time chat:* Face-to-face and phone conversations are not protected by copyright unless they are recorded or transcribed in a tangible medium. If you have an answering machine that records an incoming message, that message is fixed in a tangible medium and copyrighted. If someone transcribes a phone conversation onto paper, that conversation is protected—for both parties of the conversation.

What about online real-time chat? Typically, one or more people will engage in electronic chatting by typing in messages. As soon as you type in your message, it is copyrighted.

♦ *Sound and MIDI files:* Most new computers come equipped with sound cards and multimedia components. No longer are you limited to text and graphic files. Now you can add sound effects, noises, short musical phrases and even full recordings to your e-mail messages. MIDI files are the electronic equivalent to the paper scrolls used in player pianos and may contain an entire musical score.

With new technology comes new copyright questions. Basically, like CDs and tapes, sound and MIDI files are copyrighted. Even sound samples like McDonald's "You Deserve a Break Today" enjoy copyright protection.

♦ *Harmful and dangerous words:* Saying what you think or how you feel is a guaranteed right under the First and Fourteenth Amendments of the U.S. Constitution. With few exceptions, citizens have a guaranteed right to say what they want, when they want, without fear of reprisals from federal, state and local governments. However, speech freedoms are not guaranteed in the private sector.

Thus, for the present, messages sent through private e-mail systems are considered private domain and are not subject to guaranteed speech freedoms. Organizations and their system administrators may exercise editorial control of speech as they see fit. In some instances an online code of conduct or policy governs appropriate speech and behavior. (See America Online's Terms of Service in the Appendix.)

Although the government generally guarantees free speech, it notes some exceptions, especially the "clear and present danger" doctrine. Included in this doctrine is speech that advocates illegal, dangerous or violent activity. To qualify, speech must meet a two-part test: the speech must be geared toward inciting or producing impending lawless action, and the speech must be likely to provoke that action.[9]

Some experts think that e-mail messages and general online activity will not meet this two-part test because cyberspace acts as a neutral zone between the sender and intended audience, thereby reducing the risk of immediate lawless action. Exceptions include threats to national security and high-ranking governmental officials such as the President.

As electronic messaging technology continues to evolve, some legal authorities think that the two-part test will be easier to meet for e-mail messages. Future e-mail containing sound and video could make it easier for many to receive messages that meet the test.

If your words injure another person's reputation, including false statements about that person, your words might be labeled *defamatory*. (See the discussion of defamation in the "Rights" section.)

Can online service providers and their system administrators be liable for comments you make? Legal precedent set in *Cubby v. CompuServe* may serve to influence other such cases. The New York federal court judge dismissed the portion of the lawsuit against CompuServe, citing First Amendment protections for libraries and bookstores as "secondary publishers." As a secondary publisher, an organization can be held liable only if that organization has a "reasonable" knowledge of the defaming information.[10] However, in a libel case involving Prodigy online service, the courts found against Prodigy, partly because system administrators somewhat controlled online content.

Future decisions or legislation may clarify what happens if the organization or its system administrator is aware of libelous content but distributes messages anyway. An exception is information about public figures, who can be discussed and criticized. However, if remarks about public figures are maliciously or recklessly published without concern for truth, publishers may be liable.

♦ *Adult material:* Uploading and downloading of adult, sexually explicit material, combined with abusive language used to stalk women and arrange sex with minors, has raised a furor.

How widespread is adult material or pornography in cyberspace? Sexual content is readily available throughout Usenet, a collection of more than 14,000 special-interest public forums on the Internet. These forums are also available to private subscription services such as America Online.[11]

Can you be liable for uploading or downloading adult material? Yes. A California couple who operated a bulletin board service was sentenced to two-and-a-half and three years in jail for transmitting pornographic images over interstate telephone lines.[12]

Many claim that liability is unconstitutional and cite the difficulty of enforcing bans on the Internet, which has a decentralized network of more than 50,000 interconnected networks.

What is your risk in uploading or downloading sexual material? What makes sexual material offensive is found in definitions of what is *indecent* and what is *obscene.*

A three-part test can be used to determine obscenity of all sexual material except child pornography. (*Miller v. California,* 413 U.S. 15 [1973].) First, sexual material must offend an average person according to the selected community standard. By *offend,* the average person would think of the material as "having a tendency to excite lustful thoughts." (*Roth v. U.S.,* 354 U.S. 476 [1957].)

One online feature can help you avoid risk. Most subscriber systems offer a brief description about sexually explicit material. Therefore, a good rule of thumb to follow is to read file descriptions before downloading sexually explicit files.

The second part of the three-part test is that the sexual material must "be considered patently offensive." To fit into this category, sexual materials must be hard-core pornography. Text, graphic images, digitized images and animation may all be considered obscene.

Part three of the test is that the work must be taken as a whole to be obscene. If any part of the work provides literary, artistic, political or scientific value, it may not be considered obscene.

With the exception of Oregon, states do not protect obscenity. Indecent material is not banned by federal and state law but may be regulated, especially to protect minors (those under 18). (*State v. Henry,* 302 Or. 510, 732 P.2d 9 [1987].)

Federal laws prohibit interstate transportation of obscene material for sale or distribution. If you decide to access an out-of-state bulletin board service offering obscene material, you are at risk.

Legally, you cannot possess child pornography for even private home use. Within cyberspace, digitized images and animated sequences that exploit participating children meet the child pornography test. Organizations should be especially concerned about obscene material traversing their systems, because the online system may be seized and the organization held liable.

Pending communication legislation may offer some relief to an organization's liability when unwanted sexual messages appear on the system. Basically, only originators and not the organization or its system administrator would be held liable.

# Risk #5: How Secure Are E-Mail Messages?

## ——— Self-Assessment ———

How well do you understand risks associated with e-mail message security? Check "yes" if the statement is true for you; check "no" if it is not. By completing the self-assessment before reading this section, you will identify strengths and weaknesses and focus your study efforts. When you complete the assessment, compare your answers with the key at the end of the quiz.

|  | Yes | No |
|---|---|---|
| 1. Password sniffers are used by intruders to gain access to your organization's computer files and to your user ID and password. | ☐ | ☐ |
| 2. With existing security technology, you can be assured e-mail messages are 100% secure. | ☐ | ☐ |
| 3. Encryption is probably the best way to ensure e-mail messages are securely transmitted. | ☐ | ☐ |
| 4. More harm is done to e-mail systems by inside employees than by intruders. | ☐ | ☐ |
| 5. Personal information is okay to use as passwords as long as you change your password frequently. | ☐ | ☐ |

Key: 1. Y, 2. N, 3. Y, 4. Y, 5. N

Imagine one Monday morning as you arrive at work and turn on your computer that you are greeted by an e-mail message from the chief financial officer announcing that the organization has been declared insolvent and an emergency employee meeting will be held at 10 A.M. in the auditorium. The only problem with this message is that it is a hoax. It was not sent by the chief financial officer but by an intruder who gained unauthorized access to the e-mail system.

Such hypothetical experiences as this one happen more and more frequently. If you think your e-mail messages are secure, think again. More and more private and pubic e-mail systems are invaded by electronic intruders. E-mail messages, financial records, trade secrets, sensitive military and government information, files and entire programs are stolen or altered—often without your knowledge.

In an Ernst & Young 1994 survey, more than half of the 1,271 respondents said their firms had suffered financial losses as a result of insufficient computer security.[13] Your risks will continue to increase as you and others continue to digitize and transmit data across networks. Already, vast stores of information have been accumulated about you in massive shared databases across thousands of networks: health records, credit card transactions, banking data, credit reports, preferences and travel plans. Lurking in the cyberspace shadows are about 2,000 hackers, or information highway bandits, ready to seize your information and put it to their use.[14] Here are some ways intruders might gain access to your personal information.

*Password sniffers.* Intruders can gain access to your organization's computer files and learn your user ID and password, thus allowing them to gain access to your files at any time. Carnegie Mellon's Computer Emergency Response Team warns that tens of thousands of passwords have been stolen.[15]

*Spoofing* is another hacker's tool whereby the hacker gains access to a remote computer by forging the Internet address of an authorized system. Once inside, the hacker looks for security holes that permit the intruder to return and gain access to valuable information that is normally available only to system administrators.

Although you may never achieve 100% security, you may reduce your risks by using some of these security measures.

*Firewalls:* Software that serves as a barrier between your organization's internal network and external networks, such as the Internet. Dedicated computers screen incoming messages and allow entry only to "trusted" computers.

*Filtering programs:* Used with firewalls to prevent unauthorized incoming and outgoing messages.

*Assured pipelines:* Provide a higher level of security. This sophisticated method looks at the entire request for data, rather than at only portions like the firewall method, and determines if the request is valid. It costs around $30,000.[16]

**The 3 R's of E-Mail**

*Authentication:* Approaches that verify message senders. An example might be one-time passwords.

*Personnel policies:* Policies that educate and train users.

*User safeguards:* Include everything from acknowledging responsibility through user contracts and agreements to avoiding leaving a computer unattended.

*Encryption:* Scrambling or coding either e-mail messages or the files attached to them. Most effective when sending messages externally. A popular version uses numbers called private and public keys to encode and decode messages. Let's say you want to send a private message to Louise. After composing your message, you use a software program to change the message text into a string of random characters. The program then encrypts the message using your private key.

When Louise receives the message, the same software program in her computer uses the same technique to turn the encrypted text into its original appearance. The two messages must match to assure Louise that you signed the message and that the text was not intercepted during transmission.

Before using any encryption product, be aware that widespread use of encryption software may negatively affect business and law enforcement because it may slow down data transmission and cause files to be inaccurately transmitted.

Until the ultimate security program becomes available, you can reduce the risk of unwanted intruders. Carelessness, ignorance of risks, laziness in using personal precautions and denial of system vulnerability all contribute to computer break-ins. In fact, some leading computer security experts claim more harm is done by inside employees than by hackers.[17]

To reduce your personal vulnerability:

♦ *Use passwords that do not reflect personal information* such as your name, birth date, parts of your social security number or a family name. In 1989 a survey of more than 100 computer systems connected to the Internet revealed that 8%–30% of passwords could be guessed using only user personal information in some hybrid form (for example, using a part of your name backwards.)[18] Instead, use a combination of letters, numbers and punctuation marks. Also mix capital and lower-case letters. Alpha-numeric combinations with a minimum of eight characters help defuse password sniffer programs.

♦ *Change your password often* and do not leave a copy of it taped to the computer or your desk.

♦ *Keep your password secret.*

♦ *Never leave your computer on while unattended,* unless you have a shut-off timer.

♦ *Keep very sensitive information on a diskette* away from prying eyes. Follow a secure disk filing method as part of your overall security procedure. Always back up and store off-site important information—including programs and boilerplate documents.

♦ *Scan all files before downloading them.* Avoid downloading a file you do not recognize. It might contain a virus.

♦ *Remove personal and sensitive information from your hard drive before having your computer serviced.*

From the organization's standpoint, here are some suggestions to help secure your e-mail system.

♦ *Periodically remind everyone of security risks* and limit the number of incorrect "log-ons" to eliminate hackers making repeated guesses at passwords.

♦ *Keep up to date* on security techniques and technology and invest in security software.

♦ *Don't create an illusion of complete system security.* The more sensitive the information stored in your system, the greater the threat from intruders. Log and investigate invalid password attempts; keep users informed about attempted and actual intrusions.

♦ *Consider using physical precautions:* privacy screens, computer locks, coated steel cables to fasten equipment securely; security plates affixed to cables and equipment; motion sensors to sound an alarm if equipment is moved.

♦ *Maintain an up-to-date list of all users* and their availability to systems and directories. Limit unnecessary access to and from external networks.

♦ *Consider an automatic dialback* for those who access your system over telephone lines. This allows the computer to call back an employee for an ID check before allowing access.

- ◆ *Shut off the network after regular working hours,* a time when intruders from remote locations and from different time zones might attempt access. Designate only one computer for accepting external communications. Doing so allows you to scan for viruses and other problems before transferring information to other computers.

- ◆ *Use multiple passwords and limit access* of specific computers to a few users, especially if data is extremely sensitive.

- ◆ *Rotate backups* and keep multiple sets to safeguard information, with at least one set off-site.

- ◆ *Disable user IDs after a given number of invalid password attempts.*

- ◆ *Establish a monitoring schedule* to spot break-ins. "There are two types of computers. Those that have already had data security problems and those that are about to have them."[19] Use your record of attempted and successful security breaches to verify hacker patterns and effective and ineffective security methods.[20]

# Risk #6: Are Messages Part of an Official Record?

## ——— S e l f - A s s e s s m e n t ———

How well do you understand risks associated with e-mail storage and retention policies? Check "yes" if the statement is true for you; check "no" if it is not. By completing the self-assessment before reading this section, you will identify strengths and weaknesses and focus your study efforts. When you complete the assessment, compare your answers with the key at the end of the quiz.

|  | Yes | No |
|---|---|---|
| 1. Most companies have adopted adequate e-mail storage and retention policies to help lessen their legal risks. | ☐ | ☐ |
| 2. For U.S. government agencies, e-mail messages are considered federal records. | ☐ | ☐ |
| 3. A prudent approach for destroying e-mail messages on PCs and back-up media might be 15 to 30 days. | ☐ | ☐ |

4. Software obsolescence should be an integral part of an organization's e-mail storage and retention policy. ☐ ☐

Let's return to Sally. Sally was surprised because copies of her e-mail messages deleted long ago from her personal PC returned to haunt her. Even though e-mail can be subpoenaed and used as court evidence, few companies have adopted adequate e-mail storage and retention policies to minimize their legal risks.[21]

The U.S. government has a team working on a government-wide policy to cover e-mail storage and retention as part of its comprehensive records and information management system; however, in the interim, individual agencies must initiate their own retention and storage policies.[22] The government took notice of e-mail because of a lawsuit to block destruction of e-mail messages from the Bush and Reagan administrations. The court ruled that electronic mail records are federal records under the Federal Records Act and cannot be destroyed without formal procedures. (*Armstrong v. Executive Office of the President*, 810 F. Supp. 335 [D.D.C. 1993].)

In the private sector, no existing law requires formal procedures for classifying or storing e-mail messages. However, good judgment in light of legal issues suggests incorporating e-mail storage and retention procedures into an existing records management philosophy. How do you decide which e-mail messages are official records and which ones are "work-in-progress"? Some authorities say that e-mail messages reflect preliminary thoughts or ideas and not official organization viewpoints or that if your e-mail is mostly "e-chat"—electronic chatting—these messages are not official records.

E-mail that is backed up for long periods of time can increase an organization's legal risks because many of these messages contain informal and personal language that can be taken out of context and misconstrued, especially in court. Some attorneys feel these messages reflect more intention and clarify positions more than does the final document.

Whatever e-mail you or your organization consider official records, retain it according to the organization's records retention schedule. Nonrecord e-mail may be destroyed either after the official record is produced or at regular intervals. A prudent approach for both e-mail messages on PCs and back-up media might be 15–30 days. However, some messages may need to be archived for longer periods in either special electronic storage areas or in paper form.

A final risk to consider is storage medium obsolescence. Be sure that, however you store electronic records, you will be able to read them when you want to. In the 1970s, the U.S. Census Bureau located computer tapes dating back to 1960. Only two machines, one in Japan and one in the Smithsonian, could still read the tapes.[23]

# Risk #7: How Safely and Legally Can Business Be Conducted Through E-Mail?

—— Self-Assessment ——

How well do you understand risks associated with conducting business through e-mail? Check "yes" if the statement is true for you; check "no" if it is not. By completing the self-assessment before reading this section, you will identify strengths and weaknesses and focus your study efforts. When you complete the assessment, compare your answers with the key at the end of the quiz.

|  | Yes | No |
|---|---|---|
| 1. Using a credit card is legal when conducting business through e-mail. | ☐ | ☐ |
| 2. You can offer and accept contracts included in e-mail messages. | ☐ | ☐ |
| 3. All contracts offered through e-mail are enforceable. | ☐ | ☐ |
| 4. Acceptance of a contract becomes effective the moment it is forwarded from one mailbox to another. | ☐ | ☐ |
| 5. Encrypting a final contract and giving an encryption/decryption key to a neutral third party is an effective contract safeguard. | ☐ | ☐ |

Key: 1. Y, 2. Y, 3. N, 4. N, 5. Y

Online business opportunities present new challenges for the entrepreneur, who must figure out new ways to market products and services and find a way to bill customers for them. In fact, online marketing is bringing about changes potentially more profound than those produced by television.24

The World Wide Web (WWW) may become the largest and most accessible bazaar, available to anyone with a PC, modem, phone line and software. Today the Web reaches 3.5 million users. By the year 2000, the Web is expected to reach more than 25 million users.25

On the WWW wholesalers and retailers—even the government—offer electronic catalogs of everything from Moroccan rugs and cars to air conditioning systems. Law firms offer legal services using boilerplate documents to speed up services and reduce costs. Public service announcements are planned, as are ratings to measure interactive media appeal.

Millions of potential online shoppers can sit at their computers and shop in electronic malls. Already more than 700 electronic malls and specialty stores serve online shoppers.26

The most popular products are those that people can buy without touching or trying on—books, software, outdoor gear, collectibles and packaged foods.27 A favorite online commodity is pizza. You select the size and toppings on screen, then pay for your order with a credit card. Payment is protected against theft by data encryption. The pizza is prepared and delivered in the traditional way.28

Beneath the hype are the realities and risks of conducting business through e-mail. The risks involve using effective electronic payment systems, keeping purchasing and credit data confidential and providing adequate legal protections.

*Electronic Payment Systems.* Besides encryption, credit-card transactions can be made more secure by using systems that store card numbers on a protected computer system and never allow the numbers to pass over networks. Upon registering with the card service, consumers receive ID numbers to use when making purchases instead of card numbers.29

Other, safer payment forms of "E-cash" (electronic money) are being tested and developed. E-cash is money that is exchanged outside established networks of banks, checks and paper currency regulated by the Federal Reserve.30 An example of E-cash is digital cash, which can be loaded onto your hard drive or given in the form of a "wallet card" to be used the same as cash. Like other electronic payment systems, digital cash is protected with encryption technology to guard against thieves and snoops. However, because transactions can be untraceable, banks, credit-card issuers and the Internal Revenue Service are not enthusiastically supporting this option.[31]

Some banks are working with software companies to offer E-money accounts. Using proprietary software, customers can make purchases online. At day's end, transactions are cleared and E-cash balances are converted back to dollars.[32]

Still another secure transaction approach is supported by a group of companies known as Electronic Business Co-op. Its system will confirm user identities and streamline merchant procedures.[33]

Even though more secure transaction methods are sure to be developed, questions about government regulation and the potential for crime—including privacy invasion, money laundering, tax evasion and counterfeiting—raise serious concerns. Nevertheless, consumers are embracing E-cash opportunities.

*Controlling Confidential Information.*  Vast stores of data have already been collected on each citizen. Internet business transactions will add to this accumulation.

*Providing Adequate Legal Protections.*  Concerns about doing business in cyberspace often focus on contracts, because they are the nuclei for most business transactions. You can offer and accept electronic contracts by e-mail, which can save time and reduce paperwork. However, some contracts must be in paper format to be enforceable. Check with your attorney before finalizing contracts online.

To avoid risks with contracts that are finalized through e-mail, be sure to detail terms of acceptance, including when acceptance becomes effective. For example, say someone posts an e-mail message offering to sell a used computer. The offer stipulates that the seller will not accept someone's offer or ship the computer until full payment is received. You sent an e-mail message agreeing to those terms. When the seller receives your payment, your offer is accepted and the computer shipped. Don't give credit-card information to speed the purchasing process unless you and the seller use security safeguards such as encryption. Even then, you may want to give the encryption/decryptional key to a neutral third party.

Another contract risk is authenticating signatures. Unlike paper documents that may leave physical traces of alterations, electronic contracts do not show evidence of fraud. Therefore, a good safety measure may be to produce a hard copy of the contract for everyone's signatures.

The future of electronic commerce will depend not only on emerging technologies but also on new, more effective security measures. Electronic data interchange, video conferencing and wireless communications will require more sophisticated and reliable information security. Explored as possible security options are fingerprint recognition, speaker identification, handwriting and even facial/retinal scanning. Such identification may be necessary if online commerce is to be secure.

# What You May Do, and May Not Do and Should Question Doing with E-mail

## 1. Individual Users:

| May Do | May Not Do | Question Doing |
|---|---|---|
| Modify, distribute, transmit and make public your own e-mail messages | Disclose or intercept others' e-mail messages | |
| Waive complete or partial ownership rights through user contract or agreement | Claim ownership if messages are part of work-for-hire | |
| Negotiate level of privacy if organization permits; if no privacy provision stated or enforced, can develop reasonable privacy expectation | Dictate to organization privacy level; cannot prevent system administrator from monitoring | Acting as if privacy guaranteed or messages not monitored |

| May Do | May Not Do | Question Doing |
|---|---|---|
| Delete, back up or store on disks e-mail from personal computer<br><br>Federal employee: follow mandated retention schedule and storage procedures | Delete, back up or store messages if contrary to organization's e-mail retention policy | Assuming messages are not backed up by organization's system; sending messages that you wouldn't want made public or used as court evidence |
| Encrypt messages to safeguard content and to ensure privacy | Encrypt messages if procedure denied in user contract or agreement | Encrypting until understanding organization's policy |
| Be held responsible for irresponsible and illegal messages | Delegate total message responsibility to organization and system administrator | |
| Make fair use of information by quoting a few lines or summarizing content | Quote entire messages, books or articles without permission | Using ideas in exact sequence or format as original author |
| Use others' ideas expressed in your own wording; redistribute messages when given permission | Repost a message to another newsgroup, message base, or forum without permission | Reusing any message until terms of service are understood |
| Post an official government document, law, statute or pamphlet | Use official government documents beyond stated uses | Copying format, sequencing, comments and summaries of government document |
| Download authorized images for personal viewing | Copy or distribute images without permission | Altering or combining others' images to produce derivative work |

**E-Mail Risks**

| May Do | May Not Do | Question Doing |
|---|---|---|
| Participate in real-time chat | Record or transcribe chat without permission | Participating in real-time chat without understanding terms of service |
| Listening to sound clips for personal enjoyment | Upload or download sound files without permission; mimic distinctive voices | |
| Express your opinions and feelings | Use speech that provokes lawless action<br><br>Verbally threaten government officials or national security<br><br>Defame another person | Express opinions or "facts" without considering consequences |
| Possess adult materials for home viewing | Make indecent materials available to minors; transport obscene materials for sale or distribution<br><br>Possess more than three copies of child pornography<br><br>Upload, download or make available for downloading child pornography<br><br>Advertise, sell, exchange, reproduce or distribute child pornography | Possess adult materials without checking local community standard or state and local laws |

| May Do | May Not Do | Question Doing |
|---|---|---|
| Use a credit card or E-cash for online purchases | | Give credit card information without verifying recipient's authority |
| Complete a contract online | | Accept contract terms without knowing when acceptance is effective; accepting soft contract signature as original |

## 2. Organizations and System Administrators—Public or Hybrid Systems

| May Do | May Not Do | Question Doing |
|---|---|---|
| Intercept or disclose messages as granted under the exceptions of the ECPA | Intercept or disclose messages outside ECPA provisions or exceptions<br><br>Expect to negate all responsibility for user actions | Reviewing all messages or none at all; monitoring without notifying employees |
| Require each user to sign user contract or agreement to waive partial or complete ownership and/or privacy rights | Include illegal terms or actions in user contract or agreement<br><br>Expect user agreement to apply to previously sent messages | Arbitrarily develop user contract or agreement without considering user expectations and needs |

**E-Mail Risks**

| May Do | May Not Do | Question Doing |
|---|---|---|
| Declare e-mail system employer's property and all messages part of work-for-hire | Allow expectation of privacy to thrive without controls and then declare past and current messages are employer's property and subject to designated privacy level | Declare ownership or privacy levels without auditing current or prospective users to determine use and expectations |
| Negotiate privacy levels; develop storage and retention policies, including official organization record | Refuse legal authorities with proper legal support or warrant access to system backup information and messages; cannot refuse system information subpoenaed as court evidence | Arbitrarily decide privacy levels without regard for system protection from search and seizure |
| Expect users to take reasonable safeguards to protect the system and information transmitted and received over that system | Leave users uninformed about appropriate system and personal computer safeguards | Assume users are personally informed and knowledgeable about computer safeguards |
| Exercise editorial control of speech | Maliciously or recklessly publish untrue information about public figures | Ignoring hateful or defaming language |

| May Do | May Not Do | Question Doing |
|---|---|---|
| Upload or download information or messages with owner's permission or under licensing agreement | Make available for downloading anything that infringes on others' copyrights or is illegal according to existing laws | Allowing others to upload or download information without appropriate guidelines; allowing others to download information from external networks without appropriate precautions |
| Provide physical and user safeguards for online system | Expect users to safeguard system without alerting them to potential risks and training them to use appropriate safeguards | Ignoring attempted or successful break-ins to system |
| Plan for storage obsolescence | Predict life of storage mediums | Back up electronic messages and archive them without planning for storage obsolescence |
| Conduct business online | | Ignore developing security technology to lessen the risks of doing business online |
| Use security safeguards to minimize intruders stealing valuable financial and confidential online information | | |

# Summary

Organizations, system administrators and users tend to feel insulated against online risks, thinking that the electronic community is outside the reach of legally and socially acceptable behavior. Nothing could be further from the truth—as proven by the increasing number of lawsuits filed.

The nation's 61-year-old communication laws are being applied to e-mail cases; but the degree to which the courts and legislators will feel compelled to get involved with the issues depends to a great extent on how well the people who own, manage and use e-mail recognize and reduce the risks involved. Seven risks are particularly associated with e-mail.

Who owns the e-mail message?

When is e-mail private?

Who can legally read e-mail messages?

What can be legally uploaded or downloaded?

How secure are e-mail messages?

Are e-mail messages part of an official record?

How safely and legally can business be conducted through e-mail?

Federal and state statutes that protect e-mail interception and disclosure in a public setting do not generally apply to private e-mail systems. Consequently, owners of these systems should take care to evaluate their existing policies and procedures to avoid legal risks. Those organizations that offer both public (external) and private (internal) messaging should expecially be aware that ECPA provisions may apply now or in the future to their systems.

Businesses need to safeguard the e-mail system. Monitoring as a safeguard tool can be effective only when business and user needs are balanced. Everyone should use common sense in deciding privacy levels that can help control suspicions, minimize personal intrusions and safeguard the system. Above all, however, organizations must ensure that all of their risks are covered by an effective and enforceable policy because they, in all likelihood, will be held responsible.

Using others' messages, reposting messages, duplicating and distributing digitized images, participating in real-time chat, copying sound and MIDI files, expressing ideas and feelings and uploading and downloading adult materials have legal implications. Organizations, system administrators and users are all at risk if actions are contrary to established law and procedures.

Securing an e-mail message is necessary to protect sensitive and confidential information from unwanted intruders. Although public and private e-mail services can use physical safeguards and implement policies and procedures, the most effective deterrent may well be individual precautions. In addition, organizations and their system administrators need to alert users about risks, attempted and successful security breaches and user safeguards to protect not only the system but also individual rights. Individuals need to become informed about and accept responsibility for their actions when using electronic messaging.

Part of securing e-mail messages from possible risk is determining which e-mail messages are organization records and which are work-in-progress. Whatever the decision, and whatever the medium used to store messages, e-mail should be handled uniformly throughout a system and in harmony with other communication policies. Since technology changes so rapidly, planned obsolescence should be an integral part of an e-mail retention and storage policy.

E-mail is fueling business growth online. To maintain a positive attitude toward conducting business through e-mail, organizations and consumers must work together to secure financial transactions and confidential information. In addition, organizations, system administrators and users need to avoid taking unnecessary risks when providing financial information and finalizing contracts. Understanding the risks and taking appropriate action will allow e-mail's benefits to expand as potential and real threats are reduced or even eliminated.

## Discussion Questions

For each of the following discussion questions, apply the information you have learned in this section.

1. In the two years that Frank has been at this job, the organization implemented an e-mail system. Frank received a password and basic instructions on how to use the software and hardware, but no other training. Besides using the system for business purposes, Frank enjoyed sending personal messages. After the second year, Frank received a formal e-mail policy from the organization claiming ownership of all e-mail messagers transmitted through the organization's e-mail system. In addition, the policy limited

e-mail messages to business purposes only. Shortly thereafter, Frank was called into a senior manager's office and confronted with personal e-mail messages he had sent more than a year ago. How should Frank respond?

*Suggested response:* What Frank did before the policy became effective should not be affected by the current policy, unless Frank performed illegal acts. Before the policy was enacted and enforced, Frank could claim an expectation of privacy, since he had been allowed to use the system without direction or control. To be sure of all legal ramifications, Frank might visit with his own attorney.

2. Darla routinely has been leaving her computer on and unattended during her breaks and lunch hour. A flame criticizing a company policy was sent from her computer mailbox to the CEO's mailbox. The message created quite a stir. Darla's supervisor holds her responsible for the situation. Who is to blame?

   *Suggested response:* Both the organization and Darla share responsibility for this situation. Darla should take precautions to secure the equipment entrusted to her care. The organization should keep users informed about security risks and personal safeguards to minimize intrusions and misuse.

3. When Organization X and Organization Z completed contract negotiations by e-mail, Organization X's president signed the e-mail contract and transmitted it through Internet connections to Organization Z. Can Organization Z accept the signature as an original?

   *Suggested response:* Although e-mail contracts are valid, electronic signatures can be forged. To be on the safe side, Organization Z could request the contract be encrypted to secure the signatures or make a hard copy part of the terms of acceptance and send certified mail.

4. Organization A recently received a gateway to the Internet and will be receiving e-mail from worldwide locations. Does the organization's system operator have a right to monitor incoming mail?

   *Suggested response:* Anything coming into or going out from an e-mail system, public or private, may be monitored by the system administrator to protect the system and to assure the owner that neither inappropriate or illegal messages are putting users or the system at risk.

5. Through an e-mail message, Todd's friend told him he can get royalty-free music through the Internet. Would you encourage him to download music files for personal use?

   *Suggested response:* Any unauthorized use of copyrighted material—including sound files—can be a copyright violation. Suggest to Todd that he either seek permission for the music clips or create his own music.

6. Pam recently discovered that an article she wrote and posted on a bulletin board service is being reposted without her permission on another bulletin board for downloading by users. When she confronted the system administrator, he told her she didn't include a copyright notice; therefore, the article becomes public domain and accessible to anyone and everyone. How would you respond?

   *Suggested response:* Pam doesn't need to post a copyright notice to have her article copyrighted. The fact that it was fixed to a tangible medium, the original bulletin board service, automatically protects her original work. The system administrator cannot repost her article without permission.

# E-Mail Rights

*"E-mail is the primary vehicle for traversing the Information Superhighway. Unfortunately, users haven't figured out what are highway signs that enforce the law and what are billboards that advertise services. The roadmaps aren't really clear either. Superhighway drivers have few laws to protect them. Many are bound to get traffic tickets in the form of reprimands, terminations, and litigation before the laws are sorted out."*

Since e-mail is a relatively new technology, many issues related to it are not as clear as we would like. E-mail policy development, pending and possible litigation and enacted and pending legislation are murky areas for most people.

# E-Mail Policy

## ——— Self-Assessment ———

How well do you understand your e-mail policy rights? Check "yes" if the statement is true for you; check "no" if it is not. By completing the self-assessment before reading this section, you will identify strengths and weaknesses and focus your study efforts. When you complete the assessment, compare your answers with the key at the end of the quiz.

|  | Yes | No |
|---|---|---|
| 1. Most companies have a clear policy that states e-mail user rights. | ☐ | ☐ |
| 2. An effective e-mail audit gives valuable information about employee uses, abuses, expectations and concerns. | ☐ | ☐ |
| 3. An effective e-mail policy focuses mostly on hardware and software. | ☐ | ☐ |
| 4. System administrators should be responsible for writing a workable and enforceable e-mail policy. | ☐ | ☐ |
| 5. An effective e-mail policy should not attempt to restrict or monitor user messages. | ☐ | ☐ |
| 6. Most companies believe they have a right to monitor e-mail messages. | ☐ | ☐ |
| 7. International e-mail policies tend to be much stricter than those used by U.S. corporations. | ☐ | ☐ |

Key: 1. N, 2. Y, 3. N, 4. N, 5. N, 6. Y 7. Y

Message ownership issues are not clear. Technically, you own the copyright to any message you create, except that your employer may own any message created on company time with company equipment and resources under the work-for-hire laws. This work-for-hire area, however, is a grey area that is affected by a person's position, power in the organization and the project being completed.

To protect you, the user, and your company, clear e-mail policies need to be formulated that set out expectations between the employer and employee, especially if your messages are transmitted outside the organization. Until recently, many organizations have not been worried about e-mail policies because e-mail was perceived as an internal, informal messaging system. The Center for Information Technology and the Law at the University of Cincinnati (Cincinnati, Ohio) lists several reasons why organizations need to establish e-mail policies.

♦ Changes in organizational climates caused by information technology

♦ Increased awareness of privacy issues

♦ Uncertainty of differences between paper and electronic documents

♦ Recent proposed legislation on privacy/monitoring

♦ Increased exposure and litigation.[1]

Some of the recent e-mail publicity and litigation have caused organizations to take a closer look at e-mail issues and computer use in general, because most organizations don't have any idea how their computer resources are used. SBT Accounting Systems, San Rafael, CA, found that $100 billion per year is wasted on "futzing,"—anything you do on your computer that is unproductive for the organization.[2] Futzing could include games, personal e-mail, and e-chatting. In an attempt to stop unproductive use of computer resources and to make employees aware of their obligations, many organizations are looking at implementing e-mail policies that establish an employer's intention to monitor employee messages. The problem is that messages created in an atmosphere of fear caused by monitoring may lose their effectiveness. Workers may cease to use e-mail because what they transmit will be held against them. So how does an organization allow its employees to make effective use of e-mail and protect its interests at the same time? By providing an *effective* e-mail policy.

# Who Needs a Policy?

Anyone who provides or uses electronic mail needs a clear policy that sets the guidelines and boundaries for what the provider and user can and cannot do. The need for an e-mail policy to protect all parties cannot be stated strongly enough.

Before an effective policy can be written, the organization needs to understand its e-mail climate. That assessment is best made with an e-mail audit, a questionnaire completed by employees (users and nonusers) to provide honest and accurate information about how employees perceive and use e-mail. Some of the typical types of information found in an e-mail audit include:

+ Job functions
+ Workgroup membership
+ Types of documents sent internally and externally
+ Users with whom employees communicate
+ Wide area networks used by employees
+ Employee/management concerns about e-mail
+ Employee training that has been offered and needs to be offered
+ Employee/management perceptions of e-mail benefits
+ Perceptions of e-mail problems.

From an audit, the organization can begin to get a picture of employee uses, abuses, expectations and concerns. Even if the organization has not yet adopted e-mail, an audit can identify some areas of concern and risk before it is implemented. The areas of records management and information dissemination and retrieval need to be carefully reviewed.

# Guidelines for Formulating an E-Mail Policy

A workable policy should not dwell solely on the technology, but rather focus on creating a balance between the company's and the employees' rights and responsibilities. A policy isn't just about hardware and software. Since little, if any, legal precedent covers e-mail issues, a coalition of management, human resources, legal counsel, computer services and users should work together to develop the policy. Once created, the policy should be openly communicated and reinforced with e-mail communication training to increase the likelihood that employees will send appropriate, well-written and legal messages.

The following issues should be addressed by the organization before it considers e-mail policy development.

1. Does every employee understand e-mail language? A paper file is different from an electronic file. Establishing a common ground of understanding will help both the organization and the employees feel comfortable with e-mail technology.

2. How does the organization view e-mail? Will it be used solely for internal correspondence? Will correspondence be sent outside the organization? To whom? How will the organization's image be represented in e-mail sent externally?

3. What are appropriate e-mail messages? Informational only? Should personnel and other sensitive information be sent electronically?

4. How secure do e-mail messages need to be? What kind of security measures are available?

5. What degree of trust will there be between employer and employee? Will employee messages be monitored? If so, in what manner? Have employees been informed of the monitoring?

6. How will e-mail infractions be handled?

7. Will third-party access to messages be allowed?

8. Will e-mail messages be treated differently from paper files? How do e-mail documents become part of the organization's corporate records?

9. What role will e-mail play in information management in the future?

10. What types of documents will be sent internally and externally? How formal do the documents need to be?

11. Will the organization allow access to wide area networks such as the Internet, America Online, CompuServe, Prodigy? If access is allowed, what risks does the organization face? What benefits can the organization gain from wide area access?

12. Will the organization allow internal user groups and bulletin boards?

13. Will employees resist e-mail? If so, what measures will the company take to overcome resistance?

14. What are the interests and concerns about e-mail from the following: management, network administrator, legal counsel, human resources, union or employee groups, end users, third parties, service providers?

15. What are the costs associated with e-mail?

16. How will policies be distributed and disseminated?

## Writing the E-Mail Policy

E-mail policies run the gamut from a short message that displays on the screen to a comprehensive written policy included in organization handbooks. No one

### Figure 1: E-Mail Policy Issues

| | |
|---|---|
| Accesses and disclosures | File retention/storage |
| User groups defined | Ethics statement |
| Monitoring/listening | Personal use |
| Copyrights and licenses | Ownership of messages |
| Appropriate messages | Grievance procedures |
| Password protections | Infraction penalties |
| Illegal viewing/privacy guarantees | Message encryption |
| Misuse consequences/penalties | Relationship to other electronic messaging channels |
| Courtesy and etiquette | Unauthorized add-ons |
| Use of wide area networks | Forwarding others' mail |
| Discriminatory language | International e-mail |
| Sexual harassment | Misdirected mail |
| Distribution guidelines | Third-party use |
| Communication skills | Laws and regulations |
| File management | |

format is best. Format will be determined by how many issues the organization wishes to include in an e-mail policy (Figure 1).

No one policy covers all of these areas. Some of the issues may be handled in other personnel policies or through collective bargaining agreements. However, every e-mail policy should as a minimum:

+ Set limits of an organization's privacy policy

+ Warn employees that e-mail may be examined

+ Establish who will do the monitoring

+ Inform employees how monitoring incidents will be communicated

+ Ensure the confidentiality of personal information[3]

E-mail policies reflect the organization's culture and may be either lenient or restrictive. A lenient policy attempts to set general e-mail boundaries but does not attempt to restrict or monitor user messages. A restrictive policy tends to curtail employee personal e-mail messages and focuses on e-mail as a business tool. A restrictive policy may also specify how employees will be punished if e-mail guidelines are not followed.

No one policy is best for an organization. The organization needs to consider all the issues and decide how it will treat e-mail. Some companies, including General Motors, McDonnell Douglas, Warner Brothers and Citibank, take a hands-off approach, making e-mail completely private.[4] First Bancorp of Ohio makes e-mail completely private to help ensure employee loyalty and productivity.[5] Epson, Dupont and Pacific Bell believe that using e-mail is equivalent to making a phone call. Personal calls and personal e-mail are discouraged but not prohibited, although the company reserves the right to examine e-mail.[6] Other organizations take a much firmer stand.

As you read the sample policies, remember that the main focus of a policy is to reduce or prevent the organization's exposure to risk and liability. Some policies are much more organization-oriented than employee-oriented.

The names of the organizations from which we are quoting policies have been omitted so that we may present and discuss the policies freely. We want to give a special thank you to our advisory board members and others who have provided the policies for our use.

# E-Mail Policy #1

XYZ Corp. provides electronic mail to support its business operations. Employees are expected to take reasonable care to secure their messages. XYZ Corp. will not monitor employee messages unless it has reason to believe that employees are engaging in illegal or unethical behavior.

**Discussion:** This policy puts the responsibility for e-mail use on the end user. A certain amount of trust exists here, since the policy does not prohibit personal messages. The policy does briefly mention security, but does not give details. Monitoring is presented as an alternative, but only if employees are engaging in illegal or unethical behavior. The policy does not say how this behavior will be determined.

# E-Mail Policy #2

BBB Organization issued an interim e-mail policy in May, 1993, which appears in the administrative manual. In part, it states: "Users should exercise caution when committing confidential information to electronic media because the confidentiality of such material cannot be guaranteed. For example, routine maintenance or system administration of a computer may result in the contents of files and communications being seen . . . . network and system administrators are expected to treat the contents of electronic files as private and confidential. Any inspection of electronic files, and any action based upon such inspection, will be governed by all applicable U.S. and state laws and by organization policies."

**Discussion:** This organization is very concerned about confidential information, since much of the policy discusses confidentiality issues. The policy puts responsibility on the user to keep sensitive information confidential. It also clearly establishes that the system administrators may see files but are expected to keep the contents private. There is no specific mention of monitoring here, nor is there any attempt to restrict how employees are using the system.

**The 3 R's of E-Mail**

## E-Mail Policy #3

This example is abstracted from the Electronic Mail Policy and Guidance Document of the U.S. Marine Corps.

Guidelines. The use of E-mail has far-reaching implications in the areas of information control and information security. Improper use of E-mail could lose information currently managed per the Marine Corps records management directives and could compromise classified or sensitive information. Adherence to the following guidelines offers significant protection against those vulnerabilities:

a. E-mail may be used within the Marine Corps to exchange both individual and organizational information. Nothing in this Order shall be interpreted as limiting the ability of a receiving organizational mailbox from electronically forwarding that correspondence to a subordinate, intra-command, individual mailbox for appropriate action.

b. HQMC functional managers may publish exceptions on the appropriate use of E-mail within their functional area.

c. E-mail is restricted to official use only, as in the use of government telephone and postal systems.

**Discussion:** A military branch has a need for classified and sensitive information. This policy clearly states that mail can be electronically forwarded. It also clearly specifies that e-mail is for official use only. Organizations that handle military contracts or need very secure e-mail might want a policy as restrictive as this one.

## E-Mail Policy #4

X Corp. uses an online notification for e-mail policies. The following appears on the screen when users log on.

Caution: This system should not be used to transmit sensitive information in clear text. Your use of XMNA (e-mail) is in support of the business of X Corp. All messages and communication composed and/or stored on XMNA are the property of X Corp.

**E-Mail Rights**

Discussion: This policy hints at encryption. It spells out that e-mail should support the business and that the company owns the e-mail messages. It does not address monitoring. The assumption here is that employees should not assume that their messages are private.

## E-Mail Policy #5

Electronic mail is a company resource and is provided as a business-communication tool. Employees with legitimate business purposes may have the need to view your electronic mail message. It is also possible that others may view your messages inadvertently, since there is no guarantee of privacy for electronic-mail messages. Please use your good judgment as you use the electronic mail system.

Discussion: This policy warns users up front that their messages may not be secure and that others have the right to view e-mail messages. It does not prohibit personal messages nor does it address the issue of monitoring; so the responsibility is on the user to make effective use of electronic mail.

## E-Mail Policy #6

[e-mail] SYSM is limited to LLL business purposes only. No private use is permitted. LLL retains the right to monitor the content of all SYSM [e-mail] messages.

Discussion: This is a no-nonsense policy. The organization is taking a firm and very restrictive stance. The policy does not say the organization will monitor messages, only that it has the right to monitor messages.

## E-Mail Policy #7

Information systems, including electronic mail ("e-mail") and voice mail may be used only for company business. All e-mail and voice mail messages are Company records. The Company reserves the right to access all e-mail and voice-mail files and messages and to disclose all e-mail and voice-mail messages for any purpose. However, employees should not attempt to gain access to another employee's e-mail or voice-mail messages without the latter's express permission.

The Company's e-mail, voice-mail and other information systems are not to be used in a way that may be disruptive or offensive to others. Employees are prohibited from transmitting messages that contain slurs or other offensive information.

Violation of this policy may result in discipline up to and including termination.

**Discussion:** This policy attempts to cover several issues: the use of e-mail for company business, the retention of e-mail as part of corporate records, the right to access and disclose e-mail messages and the user's responsibility not to access others' e-mail. This policy also addresses disruptive or offensive activities.

## E-Mail Policy #8 [draft policy]

All communications and information transmitted by, received from or stored in electronic mail ("e-mail") or voice-mail systems are the property of ABC Co. E-mail and voice-mail systems are to be used solely for business purposes.

To ensure that employee use of e-mail and voice-mail systems is consistent with ABC Co. business interests, ABC Co. may routinely monitor e-mail and voice-mail communications.

Misuse of e-mail or voice-mail systems may result in discipline up to and including termination of employment. (A few examples of prohibited misuse of e-mail or voice-mail include: using e-mail or voice-mail to send personal messages, accessing or sending e-mail or voice-mail from someone else's file without explicit prior permission, unlawfully distributing copyrighted material, forwarding e-mail or voice-mail without authorization from the sender, creating or sending e-mail or voice-mail messages that could be viewed by management as offensive or a violation of the anti-harassment policy and creating or sending e-mail or voice-mail messages that are not in the company's business interests, etc.)

All passwords are the property of ABC Co. No employee may use a password that has not been issued to that employee or that is unknown to ABC Co. Employees who violate this policy are subject to disciplinary action, up to and including discharge.

**Discussion:** This policy is restrictive. It clearly establishes ownership of messages and use of the system. It sets up the possibility of monitoring and establishes how infractions will be handled. It also covers copyright, distribution without authorization, defamatory messages and password protection.

## E-Mail Policy #9

This last policy example is the most comprehensive. It clearly spells out the rights and responsibilities of the user and provider. It has often been cited by e-mail experts as a model policy.

Throughout this book, statements are made regarding the proper use of Company information resources. This section gives further detail with respect to the policies which govern their use.

Company relies heavily on various kinds of information resources in its daily operations. These resources include data processing systems, electronic mail ("e-mail"), voice mail, telephones, copiers, facsimile machines and other information-generation and exchange methods. It is very important for users to recognize that these resources are made available to them to help the company meet its short- and long-term goals, objectives and competitive challenges. Any improper use of any resource **is not** acceptable and **will not** be permitted.

The company policies listed here form the basis for the IRPP:

1. Data and information about the operations of the Company and its employees are collected and retained only to satisfy legitimate business purposes or as required by law.

2. Protecting Company information is every employee's responsibility. Company people share a common interest in ensuring information is not intentionally, accidentally or improperly disclosed, lost or misused.

3. Positive steps must be taken to prevent improper disclosure of Company information and unauthorized access to company information resources. Additional considerations apply if Company work is performed away from one's place of work or in conjunction with external organizations. The use of Company-owned information resources outside Company premises will be authorized solely as a business necessity.

4. Data, information and processing resources are Company assets which may be used only for management-approved company business purposes and not for personal or any other kinds of use or gain.

5. Like any Company asset, Company reserves the right to inspect information resources and their use at any time. Company **does not** monitor the **contents** of these resources, but does monitor systems operation levels for the purpose of gathering performance statistics so that they can be made known to management on an ongoing basis. Company also reserves the right to intervene in an e-mail or other computer account if there is a reason to believe that a security violation has occurred, if the user of the account is experiencing operational difficulty (thus requiring expert diagnosis of the problem) or if there is evidence that the user is abusing the resource. In such cases, notifying the user that the account and its contents are being examined is optional at Company's discretion.

6. Company records and information are available to individuals only on a need-to-know basis. Access or attempted access to information and the use of information resources outside one's authority are prohibited.

7. Established corporate and unit procedures are to be used for budgeting, approval and acquisition of information-processing facilities, equipment, software and support services.

8. Protective measures must be provided to control access to and protect the integrity of all information systems that process information.

**E-Mail Rights**

9. Appropriate safeguards must be built into information-processing facilities. These safeguards should minimize the extent of loss of information or processing support that could result from such hazards as fire, water or other natural disasters while, at the same time, maintaining operational effectiveness. Business recovery plans must provide for continuation of vital business functions if loss or failure should occur.

10. Independent reviews to ensure that program objectives are being met are an integral part of this effort. These reviews may be conducted by Corporate Auditing, a unit's internal audit staff or external auditors.

11. Deliberate unauthorized acts against Company or customer automated information system(s) or facilities, including but not limited to misuse, misappropriation, destruction of information or systems resources, the deliberate and unauthorized software/shareware, will result in disciplinary action as deemed by management.

From the user's point of view, some of the policies presented in this section may seem overly restrictive, but from an organization's point of view, the computer is viewed as a business tool to be used to support the operations of that business. Organizations believe that a restrictive policy may protect them from potential liabilities. For example, the Bank of Boston specifies the right at any time to examine work and output. On a routine audit, the bank found an employee handicapping dog races and running a bookie operation on the bank's e-mail system. The employee thought it was OK because he did it at night and on his breaks. The employee was fired.[7]

The need for policies is even more important for organizations communicating internationally. The European Community (EC) will establish unilateral policies for the transfer of information among the 12 member countries. The drafts make electronic monitoring virtually illegal, and prior authorization is needed before an individual's message can be transferred. For U.S. companies, the biggest problem is Article 24, which gives the EC the right to block a company's moving electronic communications of any kind on either private or public networks when the company's internal privacy policy does not meet the EC standard.[8]

# E-Mail Monitoring

Many of the policies addressed monitoring. Is monitoring a common business practice? A survey by *MacWorld* reported that 30% of companies with 1,000 employees or more say routine monitoring of e-mail messages is commonplace. The magazine estimated that 20 million people work for companies that provide little electronic privacy for its employees, and 60% of monitoring companies hide the fact from their employees.[9] However, if companies announce routine monitoring, users may quit using e-mail. A division of Hewlett-Packard saw a two-thirds drop in e-mail when they warned users that messages might be monitored.[10] Only 18% of companies who do monitor have written electronic privacy policies.[11]

# Communicating the Policy

Once the policy statement has been written, organizations must make this policy known to users, especially if employees are to have their e-mail monitored. Let's see what happened to Sally.

Remember that Sally used her company's e-mail system to send personal messages. Her supervisor, Ms. Smith, and the Information Systems Manager, Ms. Gordon, confronted her with copies of 20 personal e-mail messages sent over a six-week period. Sally was informed that she was fired because she had misused company resources. Sally was flabbergasted. She did not know the company had an e-mail policy that included message monitoring, and she did not recall being told of the consequences of using e-mail for personal messages. In fact, she had only sent personal messages on breaks and during her lunch hour.

Who is at fault in this situation? Both Sally and her company are at fault. Sally was misusing company resources. The e-mail system was not provided for her to send personal messages; it was provided as a business tool. The company was also at fault for not having a clear e-mail policy and communicating it to the employees. Sally may have thought twice about sending a personal message to Jane down the hall if a message had appeared on her log-on screen reminding her that e-mail is for company business only. To communicate the policy, the company can use:

*On-line message that appears when a user logs on to e-mail.* This constant reminder may be only a line or two, such as the online policies presented above; but it clearly keeps the policy in front of users.

*Policy statement contained in employee handbooks.* Log-on screen policy statements should be kept short, but each employee should have an up-to-date copy that defines employee risks, rights and responsibilities.

*Hiring statement notifying employees of e-mail and other computer policies.* Many organizations require employees to sign nondisclosure statements and other forms. It is perfectly appropriate for employees to sign a statement specifying that they understand and will abide by the organization's e-mail policy.

*Notices with paychecks and other company documents* that employees read. Employees need to be reminded of the policy. Reminders with important documents like paychecks will be seen by everyone.

*Training sessions on computer use and e-mail policies.* An employee who is told that monitoring will occur may be apprehensive about using an e-mail system. Training sessions where policies are explained and demonstrated can help allay fears. Organizations should explain how they will monitor and show employees why monitoring is necessary. When Nordstrom, a West Coast retailer, implemented a new e-mail system, it used multiple channels to advertise the new policy. Nordstrom sends the policy to every new user on the e-mail system; it is always discussed in e-mail training classes; it is continually posted on bulletin boards and it is published in a quick reference guide for users. Nordstrom believes that to "advertise, announce and repeatedly publish" will make its e-mail privacy policy successful.12

If employees are routinely informed of company policies—that e-mail belongs to the company, that it cannot be used for personal use, and that it will be monitored—employees have less of a chance of winning a privacy infringement lawsuit.

# Legislation and E-Mail

—— S e l f - A s s e s s m e n t ——

How well do you understand the effect of e-mail laws? Check "yes" if the statement is true for you; check "no" if it is not. By completing the self-assessment before reading this section, you will identify strengths and weaknesses and focus your study efforts. When you complete the assessment, compare your answers with the key at the end of the quiz.

|  | Yes | No |
|---|---|---|
| 1. Federal legislation protects my e-mail messages sent over public lines, like telephone lines. | ☐ | ☐ |
| 2. Federal legislation protects my e-mail messages sent inside my organization. | ☐ | ☐ |
| 3. The First Amendment protects my right to say anything I want in an e-mail message sent via an online bulletin board. | ☐ | ☐ |
| 4. All states have legislation governing e-mail. | ☐ | ☐ |
| 5. I cannot be held accountable for libelous messages sent on the Internet. | ☐ | ☐ |
| 6. The Internet is governed by specific federal laws that specify its uses. | ☐ | ☐ |

Key: 1. Y, 2. N, 3. N, 4. N, 5. N, 6. N

This section of the book offers general information about laws that affect e-mail use. It is not legal advice. Any specific questions you have about legal issues pertaining to e-mail should be directed to legal counsel.

As more information is stored electronically, an organization has fewer means to secure and protect its data. It's hard to put a padlock on a hard drive. Although the legal system is behind in defining electronic information law, some laws do offer protection; at this time, however, more laws protect the organization than the individual user.

# Electronic Communications Privacy Act (ECPA) of 1986

Most experts believe that the ECPA is the best protection users have for e-mail messages. The ECPA was developed to expand the existing wiretap laws and protects all communications in which an individual holds a reasonable expectation of privacy.13 The Act makes it "a federal crime to intercept and disclose electronic communications, in much the same manner that the wiretap statute prohibits the interception of phone calls." It also prohibits unauthorized access to messages stored electronically.14 System administrators are not free to disclose the contents of e-mail messages unless messages are sent to them. They are free to disclose the contents of messages if the sender is perceived as harming the system or another user. Users can sue if the ECPA is violated.

The ECPA does not protect users in the private workplace. The ECPA applies to messages sent only over public lines, like telephone lines. If your organization has an internal e-mail system, the ECPA does not apply to intraorganizational communications. In other words, you may not own the e-mail messages you create on your organization's equipment, send on your organization's networks or store on your organization's computers.

The ECPA provides for random monitoring, and the organization can provide messages stored less than 180 days to law enforcement officials with a signed court order. Messages stored more than 180 days may be obtained without a warrant.15 The ECPA does not provide privacy for messages transmitted to a public bulletin board, since that is considered a public forum.

Some organizations have hybrid electronic mail systems where both public service and internal e-mail systems exist. Any organization or user on a hybrid system should consult legal counsel to determine if the ECPA applies.

Some states have passed laws regarding electronic privacy. Users should check their state statutes for electronic privacy laws.

**The 3 R's of E-Mail**

Do you have any recourse if your electronic mail privacy is violated? Tort law of invasion of privacy is available, but it has serious limitations. A tort is a private or civil wrong. It may include, but is not limited to, fraud, negligence or product liability. If you need more information on these aspects of the law, refer to the Sources List in the Appendix.

Some employees have sued their employers on the grounds that their privacy was violated because their e-mail messages were read by managers. Some cases are still pending, although one case in California (*Flannigan vs. Epson America*) held that existing statutes did not apply to electronic mail.

# Copyright Act

Copyright law is federal; no state copyright laws exist. For a copyright to be valid, the work must be original; authorship must be proved; the work must be fixed in a tangible medium of expression; and the work does not extend to any idea, procedure, process, system, method of operation, concept, principle or discovery.

The Copyright Act was amended in 1976 to make it easier for persons to own the copyright on original material. Technically, you own the copyright on an original work that you create because an automatic copyright is afforded for original expression that can be fixed in tangible form. It is no longer necessary to register a copyright to establish ownership, but copyrights must be registered before you can file suit against someone violating your copyright.

A copyright allows the author to reproduce the work; create a derivative work; and distribute, display or conduct a performance of the work. A copyright lasts 50 years past the author's death if the work was created after 1977. Most e-mail, of course, falls into this category. Imagine: If you are 30 years old in 1995 and live until you 80, any e-mail message you create today is technically copyrighted to you until 2095. Some legislators would like to extend the copyright an additional 20 years. (See proposed legislation for additional information.)

E-mail messages people write at work come under the "work-for-hire" statutes and are considered commercial considerations. Work for hire means that if you create a "work" within the scope of your employment, your employer owns the "work." That theoretically means that your employer has the right to do anything with your e-mail messages that he or she wants. But the work-for-hire standard is a grey area. Employee tasks really determine if the message created on company time with company equipment and resources falls under the work-for-hire standard. That does not absolve you of the responsibility for making sure that you give proper credit to anyone else's words, images or music that you use in an e-mail message.

## Fair Use

The fair use section of the copyright law allows copyrighted works to be reproduced for the following purposes: criticism, comment, new reporting, teaching (including multiple copies for classroom use), scholarship and research. In the past, nonprofit educational purposes were generally considered fair use. Thus, a teacher could copy an article for use in a class, but could not put several articles together in a packet and then sell them to students. Recently the fair use section has been challenged by a lawsuit filed against Texaco. The Second Circuit Court ruled that Texaco was in violation of copyright law because it allowed one of its researchers to place in his files copies of articles from the *Journal of Catalysis,* published by the American Geophysical Union. If this ruling is upheld, it brings into serious question whether there is any fair use of copyrighted material reproduced by mechanical means, even though Texaco claimed the works were copied for research purposes.

## First Amendment

When people think of the First Amendment, they envision Tom Paine and other American patriots printing revolutionary pamphlets. Freedom of speech is a cornerstone of our way of life in the United States. The Bill of Rights and the Constitution are guarantees that we are protected against government oppression. However, the First Amendment does not apply to private acts.

Does the First Amendment apply to electronic mail? Walter Ulrich, an e-mail specialist, believes that First Amendment rights do not apply to internal corporate e-mail because it is viewed as commercial communication.[16] On the other hand, Laurence J. Tribe, a Harvard law professor and constitutional law expert, believes that the First Amendment will be the single most important legal document for the proposed Information Superhighway.[17] One thing is for sure—online services such as America Online and Prodigy are considered privately owned, so their administrators are free to control messages sent and distributed. (See America Online's Terms of Service included in the Appendix.) In fact, Prodigy automatically scans 75,000 daily messages for profanity or racial epithets. Messages that contain questionable material are returned to senders with computer-generated ideas about how the message could be reworded.[18]

The First Amendment permits states to pass laws restricting "fighting words"—language so offensive and abusive that it may incite the audience. Many users believe that flaming, therefore, is illegal, since flaming can be abusive. So far flaming is not illegal because the participants are not in physical proximity and therefore are not subject to physical harm. As technology advances, this standard will be less accurate—especially as sound and video add new perspectives.

# Fourth Amendment

The Fourth Amendment to the Constitution protects citizens from unreasonable searches and seizures. Again, this amendment protects citizens from unlawful *governmental* intrusion into their lives. It does not pertain to private actions taken by citizens against each other. Some experts have argued that the Fourth Amendment could be used to prevent monitoring of electronic communications. Most legal experts believe, however, that monitoring is neither a search nor a seizure.

# Defamation

Another area of law affecting the e-mail user is defamation—harm caused by false or damaging statements published to an audience other than just the plaintiff. Spoken messages are called *slander;* written words are called *libel.* In both cases, the statements must be made or published to someone other than the person defamed.

Until recently, defamatory e-mail messages have been treated as libel. With the ability to incorporate sound into electronic messages, slanderous e-mail is a real possibility.

Organizations and other entities may be charged with tort for employees' comments. Included as part of "agency principles," if an employee's misconduct is connected to the workplace, the organization may be held liable.[19]

## Internet Acceptable Use Policies

The Internet has no laws governing it other than those that govern all electronic communications. However, network hosts enact acceptable use policies that govern the use of the Internet. The laws that govern the use of an Internet host computer are the laws or policies where that host is physically located. There may be state, local or organizational policies. However, just because you follow the laws does not mean that you are following Internet policies. If you violate Internet policies, your access to the Internet could be terminated.

## Open Meeting Laws

Many governmental agencies have open meeting laws that require officials to discuss policy issues in full view of the public to prevent collusion and corruption by public officials. Recently a Colorado official tried to use an open meeting law to read and print e-mail messages sent by city officials under the pretext that e-mail falls under the open meetings law. The practice was discontinued when other city officials complained, but an interesting issue is raised. How should governmental e-mail be perceived? Does the public have a right to examine any e-mail message sent by an elected or appointed official?[20]

## Legal Issues and Pending Legislation

Several issues that may impact our ability to use electronic mail are pending.

1. Clipper

   Clipper is a $50 computer chip designed to eliminate electronic eavesdropping. It can be inserted into a phone or computer to scramble information— supposedly to keep unscrupulous individuals from intercepting information. However, Clipper has a special code that can be unlocked by authorized individuals—namely the U.S. government, which means that anyone with the key could listen in on any phone conversation or monitor any computer transmission. Most experts believe that the Clipper issue is dead, but the government may propose other devices.

### 2. National Computer Ethics and Responsibility Campaign

The NCERC is a consortium of computer companies, government officials and advocacy groups that educates the public about the social and economic consequences of inappropriate user behavior such as software privacy, electronic fraud, computer viruses and e-mail abuse. The group provides sample codes of ethics and other materials to promote responsible computer use.[21]

### 3. OMB's E-mail Policy

The Office of Management and Budget has created a task force to consider e-mail issues of electronic filing, electronic commerce and interacting with and between states. The task force will also develop a government-wide e-mail policy.[22] Some officials believe that the OMB should create an e-mail program office and an e-mail management council. Many experts believe that if the OMB does establish a government-wide policy, it will become the standard for all organizations.

### 4. An Act to Prevent Abuse of Electronic Monitoring in the Workplace

Proposed by the Massachusetts Coalition on New Office Technologies, the bill would require businesses to tell employees if they will be monitored, how the data will be collected, the frequency of the monitoring and how the data will be used.[23] If Massachusetts adopts this bill, other states will probably follow.

### 5. Bill of Rights and Responsibilities for Electronic Learners

This model computer network policy was developed as part of the Educational Uses of Information Technology program of EDUCOM. The policy addresses individual rights and responsibilities and institutional rights and responsibilities. This Bill of "Rights" puts the responsibility for ethical use on the end user, including the major issue of security.

### 6. Revision of Copyright Act

The proposal, published in a green paper called "Intellectual Property and the National Information Infrastructure," explicitly will include issues of electronic copyright. The revisions could also make it easier for persons to sue someone for copyright infringement.24

## 7. Privacy for Consumers and Workers Act

Senator Paul Simon (D-Illinois) introduced this bill during the 1989–90 term and in subsequent terms, including 1995. The bill would prevent abuse of electronic monitoring in the workplace by mandating that organizations prove that monitoring is relevant to job performance and that the work be monitored, not the employee. The bill would prohibit secret monitoring. Industry has fought the bill because it sees monitoring ". . . as a useful tool for quality control."25 The Electronic Messaging Association opposes the bill because it believes that the bill could cripple the electronic messaging business and that employee rights would be substantially reduced.26 This bill has not advanced since its first introduction.

## 8. Communications Decency Act of 1995

Senators Exon and Gorton introduced a bill that would expand FCC regulations on obscene and indecent material to cover all content carried by all forms of electronic communications networks, including all phone lines, commercial online services, the Internet and other bulletin boards. SB314 would require carriers to take steps to prevent minors from gaining access to indecent audiotext and makes harassment over interstate phone lines a criminal offense. Carriers would be liable and would be required to screen all messages and files.27 Under this act, the federal government would be required to monitor electronic mail, bulletin boards and "all other forms of digital data sent via modem over PC networks for obscene, lewd, etc., comments and proposal." Users caught posting obscene material could be fined up to $100,000 and/or serve up to two years in jail.28 This bill gives broad license to monitor and would make network administrators more responsible for the digital data sent through their gateways. Critics of the bill maintain that it imposes government-mandated censorship. Even someone who flames could be sued for harassment.

## 9. Proposed Constitutional Amendment authored by Laurence J. Tribe

Laurence J. Tribe, a Harvard Law School professor and an expert on constitutional law has proposed a constitutional amendment that would apply the provisions of the First and Fourth Amendments to electronic technology.

**The 3 R's of E-Mail**

"This Constitution's protections for the freedoms of speech, press, petition, and assembly, and its protection against unreasonable searches and seizures and the deprivation of life, liberty, or property without due process of law, shall be construed as fully applicable without regard to the technological method or medium through which information content is generated, stored, altered, transmitted, or controlled."[29]

No one really expects the Amendment to pass, but it has focused attention on the need to deal with electronic communications.

10. **HR989 and SB483—Copyright extension bills.**

Both the House (Moorhead, Schroeder, Bono, *et. al.*) and Senate (Hatch and Feinstein) have proposed legislation to extend the copyright 20 years. This bill would affect text, sound, and graphics sent electronically.

# Litigation Related to Electronic Mail

E-mail cases are just now making their way through the court systems. Some of the pending cases may have been litigated or settled out of court by the time this book goes to print.

### *United States v. Poindexter*

In one of e-mail's first tests, a federal judge ruled that e-mail messages sent by then national security advisor, John Poindexter, to Colonel Oliver North could be used as evidence in the Iran-Contra hearings. The case was important because it established that printed copies of e-mail messages could be used as admissible evidence. The court accepted the e-mail messages because a trusted recordkeeper had made a copy and retained it. By auditing system information, Poindexter could be confirmed as a message originator.[30]

### *State of Michigan v. Andrew Archambeau*

The state of Michigan has a stalking law that has been applied to e-mail and telephone answering machines. In a three-month period in 1994, Archambeau sent over 20 e-mail messages and several packages and letters to a woman he courted through a video dating service. If Archambeau is convicted, he could face a year in jail and fines of $1,000. This case may be used to advance federal stalking legislation.[31]

---

### Santa Clara Junior College Bulletin Board

Santa Clara Junior College was sued by three students over an all-male bulletin board. Derogatory and anatomically explicit messages about female students were posed on the bulletin board. The case was settled out of court with the college paying each of the plaintiffs $15,000, but interesting questions were raised about freedom of information and sexual discrimination with digital communications.[32]

### Stratton Oakmont, Inc. v. Prodigy Service Company

Prodigy provides on-line services to subscribers. Lawyers for Stratton Oakmont contend that Prodigy published inaccurate statements about the bank on the MoneyTalk discussion line. They filed a $200 million libel lawsuit.[33] A New York Supreme Court ruled Prodigy a publisher of information rather than a distributor. Prodigy was held responsible for comments posted on a computer bulletin board. 300 on-line companies are supporting Prodigy in its continued appeal. The parties settled out of court, leaving the court's decision in question.[34]

### Borland International, Inc. v. Symantec Corp.

Eugene Wang, a Borland employee, was charged with transferring files to Symantec when he resigned from Borland and took employment with Symantec. Borland obtained search warrants to search Wang's electronic files and those of Symantec employee, Eubank. This case focused on the content of e-mail messages and the expectations of privacy based on the assignment of unique passwords. The case is pending.[35]

### Alana Shoars v. Epson America Inv.

Shoars was an e-mail administrator at Epson and told employees that their e-mail was private. When Shoars learned that a manager was reading and printing every e-mail message transmitted or received, she protested and was fired for insubordination. Shoars sued for $3,000 per message on invasion of privacy, but the court dismissed the case. A class-action suit on behalf of all employees whose mail was read has been filed. The case has been appealed.[36]

### Thomasson v. BankAmerica

This case challenges e-mail privacy. Bank of America did a content search of e-mail messages and learned that a secretary had a side career as a stripper.[37]

### George Frena v. Playboy

Frena ran a bulletin board on which digitized images of *Playboy* photos were available. *Playboy* sued Frena for copyright infringement. Frena said that he was unaware of the images and removed them as soon as he learned of them. The court found in favor of *Playboy*.[38]

### Academic Sues Colleague

Laurence Godfrey, a Canadian sued a colleague for libel because he was defamed in a message posted on an electronic bulletin board on the Internet. Great Britain allows the case to be litigated if only one person viewed the message. English law, which is stricter than American law, would require system operators to prove that they had not been negligent or reckless.[39]

### Ripken E-mail "Death Threat"

Cal Ripken is a baseball player for the Baltimore Orioles. The team was scheduled to play the Seattle Mariners. Seattle officials intercepted an e-mail message on a public access bulletin board and believed it to be a death threat against Ripken. The message was sent by a young woman to her boyfriend, who is a Ripken fan. She was simply teasing him. She was not charged, but she received a bill for $700 for the extra security at the Kingdome where the Orioles were supposed to play.[40]

### American Geophysical Union v. Texaco

This case tested the fair use part of the copyright laws. In the past, copyrighted works could be reproduced if they were used for criticism, comment, news reporting, teaching, scholarship or research. The American Geophysical Union, which publishes the *Journal of Catalysis,* filed suit because a Texaco employee had copies of eight articles in his files to use for later reference. The courts ruled that Texaco violated fair use because the employee made copies for archival reasons, because the copying was not "reasonable and customary" and because Texaco is a for-profit concern, even though the researcher made the copies for research purposes. The courts believed that the magazine lost revenue because Texaco had not purchased enough subscriptions for all the researchers. This case has been settled out of court.[41]

*Meeks v. Suarez Corporation Industries*

Meeks is the author of an electronic newsletter called Cyberwire. Online he criticized the marketing tactics of Suarez Corporation Industries, a company that runs sweepstakes promotions. Suarez sued for defamation. This was important because it was one of the first libel cases involving the Internet. Suarez has been the subject of two other false marketing suits, which were both settled out of court. The Meeks case was settled out of court.[42]

*University of Illinois Freshman Threatens President Clinton*

A University of Illinois freshman used campus resources to send the following Internet message to President Clinton: "I am curious, Bill, how would you feel about being the first president to be killed on the same day as his wife . . . It would be best, I think, to not continue with your immediate plans. Perhaps a vacation. You will die soon. You can run, but you cannot hide." (Threat.txt from University of Illinois Gopher site, February 25, 1994.)

A computer trace by university officials identified the student as the author, even though he was using an alias, allmighty@never.gonna.catch.me. The student was not prosecuted, but the speedy way that the Secret Service, FBI and university officials investigated and identified the student points out that even aliases cannot protect users from inappropriate e-mail messages.

# Summary

As an online user, you have less protection in the workplace than you do at your home computer. You have less protection using an internal e-mail system than you do using a subscriber system such as America Online.

All businesses should have an e-mail policy. The policy can be lenient or restrictive, but it needs to be communicated to all users. Without a policy, everyone walks an electronic tightrope without a safety net. No ideal policy exists. The policy must reflect the organizational climate.

Many laws affect e-mail use: the ECPA, the First and Fourth Amendments, copyright laws and fair use, defamation and open meeting laws. E-mail users are not above the law.

Industry hardware and software issues, proposed user codes and legislation also will affect e-mail use. The bottom line: stay informed, because e-mail is the single most important part of today's information technology.[43]

# Discussion Questions

1. You have just accepted a position at Warner Enterprises. When you interviewed, you noticed that your supervisor was using electronic mail. What are some of the e-mail issues you would want clarified before you use the e-mail system? What questions would you ask?

   *Suggested response:*

   Does the company have a policy?

   How would I be affected by the policy?

   Does the company monitor e-mail?

   Does the company send both internal and external e-mail messages?

   What are appropriate messages?

2. Reread the scenario about Sally. What mistakes did she make? How could she have protected herself?

   *Suggested response:* Sally assumed that personal e-mail messages were okay if she wrote them on lunch hours and breaks. She also assumed that her messages were private and secure. She should have been a more informed e-mail user.

3. Do you think employers should have the right to monitor e-mail messages? Why or why not?

   *Suggested response:* There is no correct answer here.

4. Consider your own organization. What issues need to be addressed if your organization does not have an e-mail policy?

# E-Mail
# Responsibilities

"What a man creates with his hand,
he should control with his head."

—Thomas Edison

Enjoying e-mail benefits without shouldering any responsibility for its use is like pointing a loaded gun at others without regard for their safety or yours. A misguided message may not kill but it certainly can harm and leave emotional and financial scars.

Even the freewheeling Internet, which has been an open forum for everything from derogatory remarks to explicit sexual material, is coming under the fire for users' irresponsible behavior. Pending legislation targets offensive messages and proposes fines for anyone who uses computers "to annoy, abuse, threatens, or harass."[1]

Many users believe that the days of "anything goes" are coming to an end. The Internet and other wide area network administrators are monitoring messages in light of recent legislation and litigation. In response, some users and activists are dedicated to fighting for freedom of expression. Others believe these interests can be balanced.

Among the leaders in the fight is the Electronic Frontier Foundation, dedicated to "helping civilize the electronic frontier; to make it truly useful and beneficial not just to a technical elite, but to everyone; and to do this in a way which is in keeping with our society's highest traditions of the free and open flow of information and communication."[2] Since 1990, EEF has advocated that civil liberties be applied to new communications technologies. It informs members and the general public about issues and lobbies for legislation that favors online user rights. Specifically, it strongly opposes government regulation of online services.

Whether you agree with controlled e-mail access, the success of an e-mail system really depends on the people who use it. You are more likely to experience success if you accept **responsibility** for sending clear, legal, and friendly messages. Your responsibility extends to the following four areas.

# Responsibility #1: Communication Style

## —— Self-Assessment ——

How well do you adjust your communication style to send effective e-mail? Check "yes" if the statement is true for you; check "no" if it is not. By completing the self-assessment before reading this section, you will identify strengths and weaknesses and focus your study efforts. When you complete the assessment, compare your answers with the key at the end of the quiz.

|  | Yes | No |
|---|---|---|
| 1. I consider each message in terms of its unique characteristics matched with available message options. | ☐ | ☐ |
| 2. Formatting electronic messages is the same as formatting paper messages. | ☐ | ☐ |
| 3. I consider my reader first when I write an e-mail message. | ☐ | ☐ |
| 4. The most important part of an e-mail message is the message text itself. | ☐ | ☐ |
| 5. Emotion is difficult to convey in e-mail messages. | ☐ | ☐ |
| 6. I consider my reader's needs before I compose an e-mail message. | ☐ | ☐ |
| 7. I avoid immediately responding to messages that evoke intense emotion. | ☐ | ☐ |
| 8. I use e-mail not only to communicate information but also to foster good will and to stimulate creativity. | ☐ | ☐ |

> **Key:** 1. Y, 2. N, 3. Y, 4. N, 5. Y, 6. Y, 7. Y, 8. Y

E-mail messages are unique in that they are a hybrid—somewhere between spoken and written messages. Seen as a viable alternative to phone calls and face-to-face meetings, these messages contain unique qualities that necessitate making adjustments to your communication style. Consequently, many of the style mechanisms for print media specified in style manuals no longer apply to this medium. The paper mentality needs to add the electronic mentality.

Some of e-mail's unique qualities are paradoxical. Here are some examples.

♦ *Instantaneous messages, transmitted and deleted from the screen, avoid paper communications.* Once received, these messages can be fixed in paper form and widely distributed.

♦ *Quick, personal messages don't require editing or proofreading.* However, many of today's e-mail messages no longer fit into the personal category. Instead, letters, reports and memos are sent internally and externally as official documents.

- ◆ *Quick messages can easily be sent and replied to without regard for time or distance.* What may be sent quickly may not be replied to quickly, especially if the receiver does not open the mailbox or reply to the message in a timely fashion. In addition, with the number of messages received increasing daily (the average is about 50 messages per day), today's e-mail user is challenged to read, let alone respond to, the deluge of messages.[3]

- ◆ *Informal, personal and private messages.* Informal they may be, but private they are not. Since messages can be retained on back-up tapes or other storage mediums for up to five years, messages may be reviewed even though they have been deleted from a user's mailbox.

*Choose the Appropriate Channel.*   The first adjustment to make in your communication style is to decide if e-mail is the appropriate channel to use. In most cases, it is only one available option. Others include written surface (most printed documents: letter, memo, report), voice (phone or voice mail), face-to-face, fax. The Channel Evaluation Guide (pages 86–87) can help you weigh your best option.

Imagine that you are the leader of a cross-functional team working on a difficult project, which has been delayed because of personality conflicts. You have been asked to report team problems and possible solutions to all members' supervisors. Team members come from company offices located throughout the state and use e-mail through a WAN.

Look at the chart. The Xs represent the best options and parentheses contain important concerns. In this case, the channel with the most Xs is the written surface. However, concern for feelings, reactions and relationships may outweigh other requirements to the point that you decide to meet face-to-face with the supervisors or to send a written message and hold a follow-up meeting to discuss the report.

E-mail may save time and reduce phone and meeting time, but it's not the right channel for every message. (For example, should an employee receive a termination notice by electronic mail?) E-mail is perceived as highly impersonal because it is computer-generated. It lacks important nonverbal communication elements such as facial expressions, body language and voice intonation. If an e-mail message is part of the company record, emotion or controversy could be misunderstood, consider another channel.

On the other hand, e-mail is seen as a highly personal form of communication—an electronic chat. The chart can help you assess your message purpose, formality and audience. Once you are confident you have selected the best channel for your message organize your message to express your thoughts effectively.

**The 3 R's of E-Mail**

*Organize and Express Effectively.* Probably the biggest mistake writers in any medium make is forgetting that a message will be read by a real person. Composing at the computer tends to bring out the worst in communication efforts. Heighten your awareness by asking yourself these questions.

- ◆ Who is the receiver?
- ◆ Is anyone else likely to see the message?
- ◆ Why am I sending this message?
- ◆ What does the receiver know? What does the receiver need to know?
- ◆ Why will the receiver read this message?
- ◆ How will the receiver react to the message? Would I be willing to give this message face-to-face?
- ◆ What is my relationship to the receiver?

Since e-mail is different from paper-based messages, e-mail messages require a different approach to be effective. The e-mail allure is reduced time and effort to communicate ideas. Consequently, senders need to keep e-mail short and emphasize key parts of the message to ensure their message gets read.

*Message Key Components.* Almost every e-mail message contains key components that establish if the message will be read. These include the *header* (To, Cc, Subject and Attachment lines) and message area. Figure 2 explains each component and suggests an appropriate use.

Because e-mail volume may be large, receivers are taking steps to avoid being overwhelmed. Some e-mail receivers use filters to prioritize messages, which can sort messages by sender or key words in the subject line or message text. The subject line is most often used to screen messages; consequently, the more compelling you can make your subject line, the more likely your message will be read. To create a good first screen impression:

1. Be specific and get to the point in the subject line.

   *Not:* Project Report

   *But:* Update of E-Mail Policy Timetable

2. If you are requesting action, include that as part of the subject line.

   *Example:* Respond to E-Mail Policy Draft by 3/15

# Figure 1. Channel Evaluation Guide

Compare message requirements with available options. Place an X where a channel option might be appropriate. Consider hidden as well as obvious consequences.

| Consideration | Written Surface | Voice | Face to Face | E-Mail | Fax |
|---|---|---|---|---|---|
| 1. Message length (long or short, message complexity) | X (potentially complex) | | | X (potentially complex) | X (potentially complex) |
| 2. Content (positive, negative, persuasive, neutral) | X (negative elements need explanation and support) | | X (negative elements need explanation and support) | | |
| 3. Formality (format of message, tone, style) | X (formal—corporate report) | | | | |
| 4. Distribution internal/external, number of recipients | X (internal distribution to supervisors at multiple locations) | | | X (internal distribution to supervisors at multiple locations) | X (internal distribution to supervisors at multiple locations) |
| 5. Need for message permanence (sender) | X (company record) | | | | |
| 6. Need for message permanence (receiver) | X (company record) | | | | |
| 7. Need to include message as part of corporate records management system | X (printed documents more likely to be included) | | | | |
| 8. Location of recipients (local, regional, national, international) | X (recipients at multiple locations) | | | X (recipients at multiple locations) | X (recipients at multiple locations) |
| 9. Number of message recipients | X (message needed by all recipients) | | X (meetings could be held to give and receive feedback) | X (e-mail can be used because all recipients on the system) | X (all recipients have fax machines) |

| Criteria | | | | | |
|---|---|---|---|---|---|
| 10. Need to include attachments or supporting materials | X (may need to provide supporting information) | | | X (documents may be attached to e-mail messages; however, all systems may not have compatible platforms) | X (attachments may be faxed) |
| 11. Time/cost sensitivity | | X (message in voice mail boxes may not be checked in timely manner) | X (message given at one time with feedback) | X (e-mail is fastest way to notify all users but may not be cost effective) | X (fax is fast, but may not be cost effective) |
| 12. Effect on others if message becomes public (confidentiality, sensitivity of information, potential for grievance or litigation) | X (low confidentiality since internal document, high sensitivity and potential for grievances or possible litigation) | | X (meetings provide way to control confidentiality, misperceptions and feedback) | X (low confidentiality since internal document, high sensitivity and potential for grievances or possible litigation) | X (low confidentiality, high sensitivity and potential for grievances or possible litigation) |
| 13. Ethnicity of recipients | (not applicable) | (not applicable) | (not applicable) | (not applicable) | (not applicable) |
| 14. Familiarity of senders/receivers (how well known are senders and receivers to each other) | X (recipients may not know sender) | | X (recipients may not know sender) | X (recipients may not know sender) | X (recipients may not know sender) |
| 15. Security (effect on employees, organization, others external to organization) | X (individual messages need not be secured) | | X (meetings allow control of who attends and information shared) | X (e-mail allows security of message to recipients, although privacy questionable) | X (low security since openly received at each office) |
| 16. Human concerns (feelings, reactions, relationships) | | X (voice contact allows gauge of supervisor reactions and feedback) | X (meetings allow gauge of supervisor reactions and feedback) | | |

Figure 2: E-Mail Message Components

| Header | Description | Appropriate Use |
|--------|-------------|-----------------|
| To | E-mail address or screen name | Use on all messages for accurate delivery |
| Cc | Carbon copy or courtesy copy to be sent to additional e-mail addresses | Use when receivers other than original addressee need the message |
| Subject | Description of e-mail message | Use on all messages—may decide reading priority |
| Attachments | File name of additional information | Attach only information useful to main message; be sure receiver's system can accept attachments |
| Message | Main message (may be one of 50 for the day) | Target one subject only |

3. Keep subject line to 25–35 characters (the amount usually displayed on the screen).

4. Avoid using "urgent" labels to get attention. After one unimportant message, the receiver will disregard future messages tagged "urgent."

5. Don't use abbreviations, acronyms or jargon unless you know your receiver will understand them.

6. Never leave the subject line blank.

Proceed to write a brief but clear message. Usually you can put your point across in one screenful (approximately 20 lines), but what looks like a screenful to you may not transfer as a screenful to your receiver. A good rule of thumb is to keep line length to less than 80 characters; 60 characters if the message might be forwarded. Figure 3 is an example of a message that incorrectly wrapped on the receiver's screen—thus slowing down and irritating the receiver.

**The 3 R's of E-Mail**

**Figure 3: Incorrectly Wrapped Message**

I just got your message and appreciate your consider
ing me
for the position. Let me know application details as so
on as
possible. I know I have the credentials you're seeking.

The body of your message should give important information up front. Begin with your purpose, include the important details and then request action. Make sure all details relate to the message topic. Use bullets, lists and white space to highlight key information.

When you reply to a message, start with the action requested and insert the main relevant facts from the original message, prefixing them with a "greater than" sign (>) or colon to differentiate the sender's words from your own. Don't, however, repeat the entire message unless it is necessary for understanding your message.

*Choose Words Carefully.* Even when you give only the relevant facts for a single-subject message in a single screen, complete with emphasis or highlighting techniques, your message can still fall flat. The reason: poor word choice. When speaking, we express ideas one way; when writing, we express them another. What's the answer? As one writer put it, "trim the fat, not the muscle." Cut unnecessary phrases and trite expressions that clutter your meaning and over-shadow the real you.

*Fat:* "As soon as you get the information from the project team leader, send it to me, so that I can review the time schedule and projected costs. I'm not sure I can get a response off to you immediately, but I will do my best. In the meantime, do you have any idea when that information will be received? Delays will really throw this project into a tailspin?

*Lean:* "Send me the project team leader's information as soon as it arrives. After I review it, I will submit a report."

The more important the message, the more attention you should give it. Read what you write. In fact, read out loud to let your ear judge whether you've selected the "right" words. Use courtesy words, avoid discriminatory language and use a simple, appropriate close. Check spelling, capitalization and punctuation.

Proofread a printed copy if the message is more than one screenful. Finally, distribute messages only to receivers who can use the information. Distributing mass messages will overload the system, reduce productivity and earn you a bad reputation.

***Sending and Receiving Flames.*** When people get angry or upset by something they read online, they can react faster and with more emotion than they can by snail mail. These e-mail responses are blunt, even rude. If the language is strong enough, e-mail is called a "flame," an insulting, argumentative message that contains insensitive or even profane or obscene language. One flame can ignite a flame war that continues for several messages or that involves many senders and receivers. Online bulletin boards and real-time discussions are well known for their flames, especially to unsuspecting new users who ask elementary questions and fail to observe the conventions followed by veterans.

Before sending a flame, ask yourself if you would be willing to say the message content face-to-face. Should you receive a flame, consider these tactics.

♦ Distance yourself from the computer for a few minutes—or even a few hours.

♦ Relax or divert your attention from resulting emotion.

♦ Return to the computer, write your response and reread it at least twice. Put yourself in the receiver's shoes. How would you feel if you received this message? Is sending it worth negative consequences and damaged relationships? Will the receiver misinterpret your words?

♦ Eliminate abusive, insensitive, profane or obscene language.

♦ Replace fighting words with soothing words. The end result could be improved relationships. You never know when the person you flamed will be your new coworker or even your boss.

***Use Jargon Sparingly.*** Familiar, simple words are still the best for conveying meaning, yet buzz words and electronic abbreviations have found their way into e-mail messages. These words and abbreviations are called "jargon," which means words, phrases and abbreviations understood by a limited audience. Jargon can break down communication and frustrate readers. Before you decide to use jargon, be sure intended receivers will understand it. Figure 4 explains a few examples of electronic jargon.

## Figure 4: Electronic Jargon

| | |
|---|---|
| NLT: | no later than |
| TMRW: | tomorrow |
| YR: | your |
| THX: | thanks |
| RGDS: | regards |
| PLS: | please |
| MSGS: | messages |
| REC'D: | received |
| QTY'S: | quantities |
| IMHO | in my honest opinion |
| PRES | presentation |
| BTW | by the way |
| BCNU | be seeing you |
| FWIW | for what it's worth |
| FYA | for your amusement |
| FYEO | for your eyes only |
| FYI | for your information |
| HHOK | ha-ha, only kidding |
| IMHO | in my humble opinion |
| LOL | laughing out loud |
| OBTW | oh, by the way |
| PMFJI | pardon me for jumping in |
| PTP | pardon the pun |
| ROTF | rolling on the floor |
| ROTFL | rolling on the floor laughing |
| WRT | with regards to |

Another way of conveying emotional context in an e-mail message is by using character sets called "emoticons' or "smileys." Some people think this visual shorthand substitutes for missing nonverbal clues to meaning. The most common of these is the smiley, which resembles a smiling face when viewed sideways. These are used to indicate humor so that sarcastic remarks are not misinterpreted. Figure 5 shows popular smileys.

**Figure 5: Smileys**

| | |
|---|---|
| :-) | Happy |
| :-( | Sad |
| :-< | Really upset |
| :-ll | Angry |
| :-(O) | Yelling |
| :-D | Laughing |
| ;-) | Winking |
| :-) | Grinning |
| 8-) | Wide-eyed |
| :-o | Shocked |
| %-) | Happy, confused |
| %-( | Sad, confused |
| :-* | Kiss |
| :-/ | Skeptical |

*Use E-Mail to Improve Human Relations.* E-mail may foster good will and stimulate creativity throughout the organization. Consider using e-mail for employee newsletters, training sessions, employee recognition and brainstorming to generate new ideas. Emphasize the human effect and less on the technology.

# Responsibility #2: Etiquette

—— S e l f - A s s e s s m e n t ——

How well do you observe etiquette when you send e-mail messages? Check "yes" if the statement is true for you; check "no" if it is not. By completing the self-assessment before reading this section, you will identify strengths and weaknesses and focus your study efforts. When you complete the assessment, compare your answers with the key at the end of the quiz.

| | Yes | No |
|---|---|---|
| 1. I understand that e-mail has its own etiquette | ☐ | ☐ |
| 2. As a general rule, copy a sender's message in your reply. | ☐ | ☐ |

3. My e-mail address is enough to identify me for messages sent outside the organization. □ □

4. When I receive someone else's message, I immediately forward it with a note of explanation. □ □

5. By using emoticons, smileys, and other devices that show emotion, I can be sure the receiver will understand the intent of my message. □ □

6. The same rules apply for sending a message outside the organization as inside the organization. □ □

7. It's a good idea to "lurk" when entering a new discussion group online. □ □

8. I avoid posting messages unless I have something to contribute. □ □

**Key:** 1. Y, 2. Y, 3. N, 4. Y, 5. N, 6. N, 7. Y, 8. Y

Many experts note that e-mail etiquette is a matter of common sense. For example:

## E-Mail Sender Etiquette

♦ Ask permission before you forward anyone else's message, even if you are using only a few lines.

♦ Don't reply to a message unless you have something to contribute.

♦ Send messages only to the persons who need to know the information. Remember that every message you send creates work for someone else.

♦ Keep messages as short as possible.

♦ Clearly identify what is fact and what is your opinion.

♦ Limit emoticons, smileys and other devices that show emotion.

♦ Send personal messages only if your organization allows it.

♦ Do not copy the sender's message in the reply unless you need to reference specific sections. "Cut and paste" only what you need.

- ◆ Don't cry "wolf" by marking all your messages urgent.

- ◆ If you are sending messages outside your organization, identify who you are, what position you hold and what organization you represent. Don't use extended signature blocks that use graphic images and quoted material (See Appendix).

- ◆ Know your audience—both primary and secondary. You lose control of your message the moment you press the Send key. Others may copy, edit or cut and paste what you have written. Be as clear and succinct as possible and remember that your message may be sent to nonnative speakers and others who won't understand slang, idioms and acronyms.

- ◆ Be aware that you may not own your messages, depending on whether you are using your own personal computer or the company's computing resources and whether you have signed a user's agreement.

- ◆ You can and will be held responsible for what you say. E-mail messages may remain in the computer system for as long as five years. What you write may come back to haunt you.

## E-Mail Receiver Etiquette

1. Reply promptly to all messages that warrant a reply. Don't reply to messages that don't.

2. If a message angers you, react slowly. Once an e-mail message is posted, it may be impossible to retrieve.

3. Give senders the benefit of the doubt. Be courteous.

4. Consider whether e-mail is the best way to reply.

5. If you receive a message intended for someone else, don't delete it. Make sure that it gets forwarded to the intended recipient with an explanation that you received it in error. Remember that changing someone else's message may be illegal.

*Internet and Other Wide Area Networks Etiquette.* The Internet is a powerful tool, but like any tool, incorrectly used, it can cause many electronic and user problems. Some fundamental guidelines for Internet use include:

- ◆ Understand the user or discussion group before you enter electronic conversations. Reading the messages without replying is called "lurking." Follow what the experienced users do.

**The 3 R's of E-Mail**

- Read the FAQs. FAQs are "frequently asked questions" associated with many user groups. These files contain information about the group.

- Post messages to the correct user group. In May, 1995, more than 10,000 user groups were available on the Internet. Lurk before you post messages so you're sure you understand what the group covers.

- Understand the topic before you reply. If you jump in without the benefit of the entire discussion, you may get flamed.

- Don't post a message unless you have something to contribute. Your message will be seen by thousands of users and take up valuable computer space—and someone pays the cost of the message transmission.

- Understand your risks of using WANs. Be an informed user about policies and laws. Not everything you see on the Internet is legal.

- Use appropriate e-mail style when posting messages.

- Remember that you can access resources because someone grants you that courtesy.

# Responsibility #3: International Communication Effectiveness

## ——— Self-Assessment ———

How well do you adjust your communication style to communicate internationally? Check "yes" if the statement is true for you; check "no" if it is not. By completing the self-assessment before reading this section, you will identify strengths and weaknesses and focus your study efforts. When you complete the assessment, compare your answers with the key at the end of the quiz.

|  | Yes | No |
|---|---|---|
| 1. Sending e-mail internationally is no different than sending e-mail locally. | ☐ | ☐ |
| 2. The use of humor is appropriate in global informal messages. | ☐ | ☐ |

3. I have the same legal protections for my global e-mail messages as I do for my local e-mail messages.  ☐ ☐

4. I have a responsibility to make sure that the global receivers understand my e-mail messages.  ☐ ☐

5. I can legally download any information that is available globally on wide area networks.  ☐ ☐

> **Key:** 1. N, 2. N, 3. N, 4. Y, 5. N

Sending e-mail internationally is one of the fastest, easiest and least expensive ways to communicate. Soon you will be able to expand international mail vertically as well as horizontally. Continental Airlines passengers will have access to the Internet on selected flights before the end of 1995.4

Even though the United States remains the leader in the global electronic community with 32 PCs per 100 citizens, other countries are catching up.5 Although sending e-mail from the United States to distant points on the globe is easy, communicating effectively is not, because every country retains its unique cultural and language differences. In addition, many countries, even close neighbors like Canada, are both more open and more self-regulating than the United States. Other countries' laws may be more stringent than ours and may become the world standard. To help you cross language and cultural barriers as the world becomes more connected, here are some guidelines to follow.

♦ Be sensitive to alternative date formats.

   European: 15 March 1995

   Japanese: 95 March 15

♦ Refer to a 24-hour clock (military time) when sending e-mail internationally and use the date.

   United States: "Please reply no later than 2:30 p.m. today."

   Military:     "Please reply no later than 14:30 on 12 December."

♦ Use metric measurements with the U.S. customary system equivalent in parentheses.

   "I drive 16 kilometers (10 miles) to work daily."

♦ Avoid using brand-name words that have become associated with general terms.

   *No:* "If I send you the file, can you Xerox the pages for others to review?"

   *Yes:* "If I send you the file, can you copy the pages for others to review?"

♦ Use the names of specific geographic regions rather than general locations.

   *No:* "I just moved to the South."

   *Yes:* "I just moved to Memphis, Tennessee."

♦ Avoid jargon, buzz words, emoticons, smileys and other electronic short-hand that a global receiver may not understand.

   *No:* Hi there, Friend, BTW, I've had the most extraordinary experience. IMHO it ranks as the Eighth Wonder of the world (;-).

   *Yes:* "Hello. By the way, I've had the most extraordinary experience. In my opinion, it is one of the most memorable of my life."

♦ Refrain from humor, sarcasm, opinionated statements and blunt language. Some common terms in the English language may have different connotations globally (for example "boot" in England refers to the trunk of a car). The more important the message, the more time you need to take to research language and cultural differences that can sabotage communication.

♦ Understand international business relationships. Outside the United States, most nations expect to establish relationships long before they do business. In addition, they may request you work through a trusted intermediary. The "Ugly American" stereotype propagates itself when people send e-mail globally in the same informal, blunt manner they do within the United States.

♦ Avoid assuming that trademarks, patents, copyrights and other legal protections are honored outside U.S. borders. Ask before leaping into the intellectual property unknown. In much of the world, laws have not kept pace with technology. In India, communications legislation was written in the 19th century.[6] By contrast, Germany has the most powerful data privacy legislation in Europe.[7]

What may be legal globally may not be legal within U.S. borders. Recent court decisions suggest that if you download something that is legal in the place it was uploaded (another state or country), it may be considered illegal according to the standards of the geographic area where it is downloaded.

**E-Mail Responsibilities**

Countries will cooperate with each other to uphold the law. In one case, the Finnish police, acting on a complaint from the Church of Scientology in Los Angeles, served a search-and-seize warrant on an e-mail remailer (someone who helps ship data around the world in complete anonymity), demanding the remailer turn over a user's name. The user's computer was used to send all sorts of contraband—from copyrighted materials to stolen software to pornography.[8]

# Responsibility #4: Preparation for Future Technology

## —— Self-Assessment ——

How well are you prepared to send effective e-mail messages with new technologies? Check "yes" if the statement is true for you; check "no" if it is not. By completing the self-assessment before reading this section, you will identify strengths and weaknesses and focus your study efforts. When you complete the assessment, compare your answers with the key at the end of the quiz.

|  | Yes | No |
|---|---|---|
| 1. Using a WAN compromises my organization's computer system. | ☐ | ☐ |
| 2. When I communicate on a WAN, I need to know how the message is routed. | ☐ | ☐ |
| 3. On a WAN, I am able to send only text files. | ☐ | ☐ |
| 4. The Internet is the only WAN available. | ☐ | ☐ |
| 5. Mosaic is a World Wide Web browser. | ☐ | ☐ |
| 6. Whether business or personal, I own my e-mail messages. | ☐ | ☐ |
| 7. Most home computer systems can easily handle graphics and sound files available on the Internet. | ☐ | ☐ |
| 8. I can create a home page to store my e-mail messages. | ☐ | ☐ |

Key: 1. N, 2. Y, 3. N, 4. N, 5. Y, 6. N, 7. N, 8. N

One of the most exciting aspects of computer technology is moving from an internal electronic communication system to a global or a WAN system. The Internet is a collection of WANs linked together. With a WAN, you can communicate as easily with someone in Chicago as with someone in Ceylon. The wonder of WANs is that the user doesn't have to worry about how the message is sent. The networking system routes the message until the message reaches the correct destination.

Until recently, wide area networks were text-based. Text files could be transferred from one computer system to another. We are entering a whole new era of computing with the ability to transfer not only text files but also sound and graphics.

The National Center for Supercomputing (NCSA) has introduced Mosaic, software that allows the user to access hypermedia resources through a graphical user interface such as Windows. Mosaic is a World Wide Web (WWW) browser. Users can access still images such as photographs or paintings, motion pictures and sound. Imagine that you are sitting at your desk putting together a plan for a new manufacturing plant in Bolivia. As part of your proposal, you could access the Internet through Mosaic and pull into your document flat maps, three-dimensional topographical maps, still pictures of the proposed plant site, video pictures of the proposed site and even the sights and sounds of the native culture. All of this without leaving your desk chair.

Your company could also create a home page—a hyperlinked document with embedded commands that allows the user to move from one document to another. For example, your home page might include an introduction to your organization with pictures of your subsidiaries. By pointing and clicking on one of the picture captions, the user could then move to a document about your distribution center in Memphis, Tennessee. That might lead the user to point and click on a home page about cultural and sightseeing activities in Memphis. That could lead the user to an electronic tour of Graceland, Elvis Presley's home, complete with video and samples of Elvis's greatest hits. Using graphics, video and sound is creative and challenging as long as the elements are properly used.

Other issues to consider include:

1. Use of graphics and sound in messages requires sophisticated computer software and hardware. Many message receivers may not have the capability to receive a message that incorporates these advanced features. Your message may be delivered garbled or not at all.

2. Transmitting and storing graphics and sound requires more computer resources. A sophisticated graphic can take more than one million bytes to store. Think about what that does to an already burdened computer system.

3. Just because a graphic or sound bit is available electronically does not mean that it is free for anyone to use. Copyright laws protect the author or creator.

## Summary

E-mail affords users many benefits, but it also carries heavy responsibilities. The ability to send messages to millions of readers with the touch of the Enter key opens the user and the user's organization to potential security and litigation problems. By following a few simple rules, users can become responsible e-mailers.

- Adjust your communication style. E-mail is not always the most appropriate medium to use. The Channel Evaluation Guide can assist you.

- Organize and express yourself effectively. Consider the receiver and others who may see the message.

- Carefully compose critical message components—To, Cc, Subject Line, Attachments and the Message. The most critical part of the message is the subject line that informs the reader of the message intent. The message should be succinct—beginning with the purpose, following up with important details and then requesting action.

- Discard all unnecessary words and phrases and give the message the same polish you would use for written documents.

- Don't send flames. If you receive a flame, give the message time and distance. Consider the consequences.

- Use jargon, abbreviations, acronyms and smileys sparingly, because they can inhibit the ability to understand the message.

- Use e-mail to improve relationships. Remember, a live person is at the other end of the communication lines.

- Be a courteous user by following the sender and receiver etiquette guidelines. Follow the role of experienced users when you use wide area networks.

- International messages require that you be sensitive to language and cultural differences.

- Hypertext allows users to create home pages on wide area networks, but may require more sophisticated systems than are available to the masses.

E-mail users need to take individual responsibility to adjust communication style, observe etiquette, communicate effectively globally and prepare for the future. If we don't, we open the door for government officials and law enforcement agencies to make decisions for us.

# Discussion Questions

1. **Scenario:** You are a human resources director in a large company and think your company would benefit from adopting flextime. The president has the power to make the change but will not act unless the executive committee supports the program. Using the Channel Evaluation Guide on the following pages, decide which communication channel will be most effective in persuading members of the committee, who are located in distant locations, to endorse your program. Consider both obvious and hidden consequences.

2. Analyze the following e-mail message. What problems can you find?

---

TO:      Team Members

FROM:  Jim

DATE:   June 1, 199X

RE:      Next Meeting—Urgent

Don't forget about the next meeting. We need to get together to decide about the agenda for the July systems meeting, which as you know, will be held in Denver. Mary called me about doing a small PRES on the status of the C. plant. We may have photographs and site maps by then that could be digitized if someone has time to work on it. The meeting may turn out to be a nasty one if we are going to ask that Joe be removed from the team. Please come up with a list of things you want to use as reasons why he should be removed. We also need to consider the team make up. Do we need a member from Accounting? What about from Marketing?

BTW, THE LAST PROJECT BUDGET SUMMARY WAS 10% OVER WHERE WE SHOULD BE AT THIS POINT. PLS come prepared to justify the over expenditures.

Also, NLT TMRW please send me the projected completion time for the ACWMNTR project. JO wants the Gantt chart by next Wednesday.

J. :-)

---

Key: Responsibility  Discussion Questions    Channel Evaluation Guide

| Consideration | Channel | | | | |
|---|---|---|---|---|---|
| | Written Surface | Voice | Face to Face | E-Mail | Fax |
| 1. Message length (long or short, message complexity) | X (potentially complex) | | | X (potentially complex) | X (potentially complex) |
| 2. Content (positive, negative, persuasive, neutral) | X (benefits need explanation and support) | | X (benefits need explanation and support) | | |
| 3. Formality (format of message, tone, style) | X (formal—corporate report) | | | | |
| 4. Distribution internal/external, number of recipients | X (internal distribution to executive committee) | | | X (executive committee networked as a user group) | X (executive committee reached easily by fax in remote locations) |
| 5. Need for message permanence (sender) | X (company record) | | | | |
| 6. Need for message permanence (receiver) | X (company record) | | | | |
| 7. Need to include message as part of corporate records management system | X (printed documents more likely to be included) | | | | |
| 8. Location of recipients (local, regional, national, international) | X (recipients at same location) | | | X (recipients networked at same location) | X (recipients easily reached by fax in remote locations) |
| 9. Number of message recipients | X (message needed by all recipients) | | X (a meeting could be held to persuade) | X (e-mail can be used because all recipients on the system) | X (fax can be used because all recipients easily reached at remote locations) |

| | | | | | |
|---|---|---|---|---|---|
| 10. Need to include attachments or supporting materials | X (may need to provide supporting information) | | | X (documents may be attached to e-mail messages; however, all department systems may not have compatible platforms) | X (documents may be attached to fax messages; however transmission cost may be prohibitive) |
| 11. Time/cost sensitivity | | X (message in voice mail boxes may not be checked in timely manner) | X (message may be given at one time with feedback) | X (e-mail is fastest way to notify all users but may not be cost effective) | X (fax messages may be sent quickly but not be cost effective) |
| 12. Effect on other if message becomes public (confidentiality, sensitivity of information, potential for grievance or litigation) | X (low confidentiality since internal document) | | X (meetings provide way to control confidentiality, misperceptions and feedback) | X (low confidentiality since internal document) | X (low confidentiality since messages arrived in open areas) |
| 13. Ethnicity of recipients | (not applicable) | (not applicable) | (not applicable) | (not applicable) | (not applicable) |
| 14. Familiarity of senders/receivers (how well known are senders and receivers to each other) | X (recipients may not know sender) | | X (recipients may not know sender) | X (recipients may not know sender) | X (recipients may not know sender) |
| 15. Security (affect on employees, organization, others external to organization) | X (individual messages need not be secured) | | X (meetings allow control of who attends and information shared) | X (e-mail allows security of message to recipients, although privacy questionable) | X (low security since openly received at each office) |
| 16. Human concerns (feelings, reactions, relationships) | | X (voice contact allows gauge on supervisor reactions and feedback) | X (meetings allow gauge of supervisor reactions and feedback) | | |

Comments: The option with the greatest number of X's is the written surface. However, since nonverbal communication is vital to the success of your efforts, you may want to prepare a written memo with supporting material and ask to be put on the agenda of the next executive meeting to present your program and answer questions.

**E-Mail Responsibilities**

*Suggested Response:* Did you find all the problems in this e-mail message? List what you found.

*Message problems:*

1. Message not specific

2. Action not requested in subject line

3. Doesn't follow purpose, detail, action approach

4. Key information not highlighted

5. Message needs editing

6. E-mail may not be appropriate channel for negative information about Joe

7. Shouting with capital letters should be avoided

8. Last paragraph difficult to understand

9. Too many different topics in one message

3. **Scenario:** Write a reply to the following flaming message.

---

Dear Top-Dog Complainer (Ms. Smith)

GET OFF YOUR SOAP BOX AND DROP THE PERSECUTION COMPLEX. You can't always have your own way when it comes to making decisions for the team. I'll bet at night you get online as poorme@leftout.com.

If you want support for your ideas, then show benefits first. When was the last time you really contributed something of value to the team? You like to take but seldom contribute.

Wake up and smell reality, sweetie. It's survival of the fittest out there, and you don't seem at all fit to survive. Why not give the team a break; resign and go pester someone else.

—Team vigilante

---

*Suggested Response:*

> Dear Team vigilante:
>
> Everyone is entitled to his or her opinion, and you have obviously expressed yours. If you have concerns about my team participation please air those concerns *openly* at the next team meeting on Friday. I do not wish to compete for one-upmanship in flaming on the network.
>
> —Ms. Smith

4. Refer to the message in discussion question two. Rewrite the message to be more effective.

*Suggested Response:*

> TO:     Janney Parker (jparker)
>
>          Bob Meredith (bmered)
>
>          Gloria Ott (gott)
>
>          Fred Jones (fjones)
>
> FROM:  Jim Logan (jlogan), Project Leader
>
> DATE:  June 1, 199X
>
> RE:     Agenda for 6/10/9X Team Meeting
>
> 1. Setting agenda for July systems meeting in Denver
>
> 2. Status of Cincinnati plan (presentation by Mary Gilbert)
>
> 3. Discussion of makeup of systems team
>
> 4. Analysis of cost overruns on project budget

**E-Mail Responsibilities**

5. **Scenario:** Rewrite the following international e-mail message to communicate effectively to a company you have been doing business with for some time.

> Hi there, Amigo:
>
> We've got a great bargain for you! You'd be hard-pressed to find a better deal anywhere on this crazy planet.
>
> Just send a quick reply to the attached offer and we'll put everyone under the gun to meet your production deadlines.:-)
>
> Joe Davis, Marketing Rep

*Suggested Response:*

> Senor Romero:
>
> Marcus Enterprises has an outstanding offer that, based on our past business with you, will reduce your production costs as it increases your profits.
>
> Please review the attachments for details. This offer will expire within 10 days or until the materials have been sold.
>
> Thank you for your continued business.
>
> —Joseph Davis, Marketing Representative

 **In Closing**

It would be easy, after reading this book, to take a negative attitude about e-mail. After all, you have read case after case where e-mail has gotten users in trouble. It seems like we have concentrated on the negative. That was not our intent, but we needed to use those e-mail abuses to point out just how important it is to be an informed e-mail user.

In fact, our hope is that you will see the many possibilities of e-mail for both work and pleasure. E-mail is such a powerful tool that to use it without the necessary knowledge and background would be foolish. Ignorance of the laws affecting e-mail does not protect you, but *knowledge* does.

Now that you have learned about the risks, rights and responsibilities, you can reap the rewards. E-mail is a wonderful productivity tool—linking you to coworkers and others across the office, across town or across the globe. We've made tremendous friends through e-mail and even managed to write a significant part of this book by e-mailing each other and our advisory board.

Take a deep breath and give e-mail a try. Let us know what you think. What's happening with e-mail in your organization? Our e-mail addresses are in the "About the Author" section. We'd love to hear from you.

Good luck and successful e-mailing.

Diane Hartman
Karen Nantz
Fall, 1995

# Appendix

# Sample Signature Blocks

Swoman

```
( )/          Mary Smith
( )= = = =     (Quilty in the First Degree)
( )\
               email: msmith@more.gov.us
```

```
= = = = = = = = = = = = = = = = = = = = = = = =
:     James B. Brown                      :
:     REPLY TO: bbrown@atlas.geo.gov      :
= = = = = = = = = = = = = = = = = = = = = = = =
```

John Doe

```
---------------------------------------------
```
All opinions expressed are my own, not those of my employer. However, if they weren't, I would rapidly be unemployed!
```
---------------------------------------------
```

After a hard day, it's nice to come home to a warm cat.
mary@abccorp.com

# Summary of Electronic Messaging Survey CPS® Seminar, June 1994

by Diane B. Hartman, ADCOMS
and Dr. Karen Nantz, Eastern Illinois University

During the three-day seminar, 317 of 373 attendees completed the survey. Ten industries were represented, the largest being manufacturing. Eighty-one percent of the respondents are administrative/executive assistants or secretaries. All are CPS holders or candidates. Sixty-seven percent are employed in companies with 1,000–10,000 employees. Eighty-three percent use e-mail, and 58.12% of that 83% have used e-mail for three or more years.

## Findings

♦ E-mail is second only to the fax in electronic messaging.

♦ E-mail is used by most as an internal, informal, information tool—with the memo being the most often used format.

♦ Most (58%) use e-mail for business only; however, 41% use e-mail for business and personal messages. Personal uses range from jokes to family letters.

♦ Most companies do not have a written policy. Where one exists, policies set guidelines for hardware and software, file retention and security.

♦ Most (72%) respondents are not connected to wide area networks.

♦ Most (69%) do not know if e-mail is being misused.

♦ Most (65%) do not receive incentives to use e-mail.

♦ When asked about training, 77% said they receive training. When focus group members (23) were asked in telephone interviews what kind of training they receive, respondents answered mostly equipment and software training.

♦ The top three advantages to e-mail include communication speed, simultaneous distribution, paper reduction and prompt messages.

♦ The top three disadvantages include increased message load, increased errors and lack of security.

## Conclusions

◆ E-mail use will continue as respondents see more advantages than disadvantages.

◆ E-mail will continue as an internal, informal information tool.

◆ Management has taken a reactive approach to e-mail and will probably continue to do so. Several focus group members said that management's attention is focused on system migration to a standardized companywide system. Management assumes employees will use e-mail properly if the hardware and software is provided and is therefore leaving proper use decisions to them. However, employees appear unaware of the scope and human impact of this technology as they make decisions about content, format and style.

◆ Businesses will slowly enter the Information Highway, especially since efforts are focused on system migration.

◆ E-mail training will continue to focus on equipment and software needs, rather than on e-mail communication training.

# America Online's Terms of Service

1. General

1.1 The America Online Service ("AOL Service"), operated by America Online, Inc. ("AOL Inc."), is a computer online, interactive information, communication and transaction service. The AOL Service is available to an authorized member (hereinafter referred to as "Member," "Members," when used collectively or "You") through a personal membership account ("Membership"); it is accessible through a personal computer, or other access device, using AOL Software (e.g. the software used to connect to the AOL Service) and a communications connection (e.g., modem, telephone line).

1.2 Please read this document carefully. Please also read the "Rules of the Road." This document, the Rules of the Road, and the "Membership Conditions" (which you saw when You first signed on) are all of the applicable AOL Service rules. (They collectively comprise the contract between AOL Inc. and Members and are collectively referred to as the "Terms of Service" or "TOS"). You can view all of these documents on the AOL Service at any time free of charge in the "Members' Online Support" department located within the "Member's Services" Area.

1.3 BY COMPLETING THE ENROLLMENT PROCESS AND USING THE AOL SERVICE AND AOL SOFTWARE (OTHER THAN THE TOS AGREEMENT AND THE RULES OF THE ROAD FOR THE FIRST TIME), YOU AGREE TO BE LEGALLY BOUND AND TO ABIDE BY THE TERMS OF SERVICE, JUST AS IF YOU HAD SIGNED THIS AGREEMENT. If you do not wish to be bound by our TOS, You may not continue to use the AOL Service and AOL Software. In that case, You should immediately terminate your Membership account and You are prohibited from using AOL Software.

1.4 AOL Inc. may modify its TOS at any time and in any manner. Any modification is effective immediately upon either a posting on the AOL Service, electronic mail, or conventional mail. If any modification to the TOS is unacceptable to You, You may immediately terminate your Membership as provided in Section 8 below. YOUR CONTINUED USE OF THE AOL SERVICE FOLLOWING MODIFICATION TO THE TOS SHALL BE CONCLUSIVELY DEEMED AS ACCEPTANCE OF SUCH MODIFICATION.

1.5 The Terms of Service Agreement, Rules of the Road and the Membership Conditions together constitute the entire and only agreement between AOL Inc. and Member with respect to the AOL Service and AOL Software. AOL Inc. may discontinue or alter any aspect of the AOL Service, including, but not limited to (i) restricting the time of availability, (ii) restricting the availability and/or scope of the AOL Service for certain platforms (i.e., computer types and operating systems), (iii) restricting the amount of use permitted, and (iv) restricting or terminating any Member's right to use the AOL Service, at AOL Inc.'s sole discretion and without prior notice or liability. AOL Inc. reserves the right to change or add any fees or surcharges at any time effective upon thirty (30) days' prior notice.

2. **Member Responsibilities**

2.1 Connect Charges.

Member is responsible for all charges (e.g., telephone) associated with connecting to the AOL Service through an available access number. THE

ACCESS NUMBER IS USUALLY, BUT NOT ALWAYS, A LOCAL TELE-PHONE CALL. Please read Section 2.A (ii) of the Rules of the Road for a more detailed explanation of telephone charges or search "Local Access Number" under the "Help" menu. To find additional or closer access numbers use keyword "Access."

2.2   Equipment.

Member is responsible for obtaining or providing all telephone access lines, telephone and computer equipment (including modem), or other access device, necessary to access the AOL Service.

2.3   Registration.

MEMBER CERTIFIES TO AOL INC. THAT HE/SHE IS AN INDIVIDUAL (E.G., NOT A CORPORATION) AND AT LEAST EIGHTEEN (18) YEARS OF AGE. AOL Inc. may, at its discretion, enter into special billing arrangements with employers and other entities. A minor's parent or legal guardian may authorize a minor's use of Member's account under adult supervision and with assumption of all liabilities resulting from minor's use. (Please refer to Section 2.B of the Rules of the Road). MEMBER AGREES TO PROVIDE AOL INC. WITH ACCURATE, COMPLETE, AND UPDATED INFOR-MATION REQUIRED BY THE REGISTRATION TO THE AOL SERVICE ("Member Registration Data"), including Member's legal name, address, telephone number(s), and applicable payment data (i.e., credit card number and expiration date or checking account information). Member agrees to notify AOL Inc. within thirty (30) days of any changes in Member Registration Data. Failure to comply fully with this provision may result in immediate suspension or termination of your right to use the AOL Service.

2.4   Accounts/Charges/Payment.

(a) Accounts.

The TOS applies to all sub-accounts and alternate screen names associated with Member's principal account(s) ("Master Account(s)"). Each Member is responsible for all activities and charges resulting from use of Member's Master Account(s) under any screen name of the Master Account(s) by any person, and for ensuring full compliance with the TOS by all users of his/her Master Account(s). AOL Service Master Account(s) may not be transferred without prior written approval from AOL Inc. and is subject to any limits established by AOL Inc.

(b) Passwords.

Upon enrollment as a Member, You will select a unique password. Member is responsible for maintaining the confidentiality of his/her password and is liable for any harm resulting from disclosing or allowing disclosure of any password. In the event of a breach of security, Member will remain liable for any unauthorized use of the AOL Service until Member notifies AOL Inc. by calling 1-800-827-6364.

(c) Payment.

Current rates for using the AOL Service may be obtained by calling Customer Service or by using keyword "Billing." Member will pay all sales, use, value-added, personal property or other governmental tax or levy imposed on the goods or services billed to his/her Master Account(s), other than taxes based on net income or profits of AOL Inc. If AOL Inc. does not receive the full amount of Member's AOL Service account balance within thirty (30) days of invoice date, an additional 1.5% (or the highest amount allowed by law, whichever is lower) per month late charge will be added to Member's bill and shall be due and payable. Member shall also be liable for all attorney and collection fees arising from AOL Inc.'s efforts to collect any unpaid balance of Member's Master Account(s).

2.5   Online Conduct.

Any conduct by a Member that in AOL Inc.'s discretion restricts or inhibits any other Member from using or enjoying the AOL Service will not be permitted. Member agrees to use the AOL Service only for lawful purposes. Member is prohibited from posting on or transmitting through the AOL Service any unlawful, harmful, threatening, abusive, harassing, defamatory, vulgar, obscene, profane, hateful, racially, ethnically or otherwise objectionable material of any kind, including, but not limited to, any material which encourages conduct that would constitute a criminal offense, give rise to civil liability or otherwise violate any applicable local, state, national or international law.

2.6 Content

(a) Proprietary Rights.

Member acknowledges that the AOL Service contains information, software, photos, video, graphics, music, sounds or other material (collectively, "Content") that are protected by copyrights, trademarks, trade secrets or other proprietary rights, and that these rights are valid and protected in all forms, media and technologies existing now or hereinafter developed. All Content is copyrighted as a collective work under the U.S. Copyright laws, and AOL Inc. owns a copyright in the selection, coordination, arrangement and enhancement of the Content, in whole or in part. If no specific restrictions are displayed, Member may make copies of portions of the Content, including copyrighted material, trademarks, or other proprietary materials, provided that the copies are made only for Member's personal use and that Member maintains any notices contained in the Content such as all copyright notices, trademark legends or other pro-prietary rights notices. Except as provided in the preceding sentence or as permitted by the fair use of privilege under the U.S. Copyright laws (see e.g. 17 U.S.C. Section 107), You may not upload, post, reproduce, or distribute Content protected by copyright, or other proprietary right, without obtaining permission of the copyright owner. Use of any software Content shall be governed by the software license agreement accompanying such software or, if none exists, then such use shall be proscribed by the terms governing licensing and use of the AOL Software as provided in Section 6 herein.

(b) Distribution/Uploading of Third Party Content.

Member may upload to the software files or otherwise distribute on the AOL Service only Content that is not subject to any copyright or other proprietary rights protection (collectively, "Public Domain Content"), or Content in which the author has given express authorization for online distribution. Any copyrighted Content submitted with the consent of a copyright owner should contain a phrase such as "Copyright owned by [name of owner]; Used by Permission." The unauthorized submission of copyrighted or other proprietary Content constitutes a breach of the TOS and could subject You to criminal prosecution as well as personal liability for damages in a civil suit. Remember You, not AOL Inc. or its independent contractors, are liable for any damage resulting from any infringement of copyrights, proprietary rights, or any other harm arising from such submission. By submitting Content to any "Public Area" (Public Area(s) are those areas of the rooms, message boards, and file uploads) You automatically grant, or warrant that the owner of such Content has expressly granted, AOL Inc. the royalty-free, perpetual, irrevocable, non-exclusive right and license to use, reproduce, modify, adapt, publish, translate and distribute the Content (in whole or part) worldwide and/or to incorporate it in other works in any form, media, or technology now known or hereafter developed for the full term of any copyright that may exist in such Content. You also permit any Member to access, view, store or reproduce the Content for that Member's personal use. Subject to this grant, the owner of Content placed on the AOL Service retains any and all rights which may exist in such Content.

(c) Export.

The U.S. export control laws regulate the export and re-export of technology originating in the United States. This includes the electronic transmission of information and software to foreign countries and to certain foreign nationals. Member agrees to abide by these laws—including but not limited to the Export Administration Act, the Arms Export Control Act and their implementing regulations—and not to transfer, by electronic transmission or otherwise, any Content derived from the AOL Service to either a foreign national or a foreign destination without first obtaining any required government authorization. Member further agrees not to upload to the AOL Service any data or software that cannot be exported without prior written government authorization, including, but not limited to, certain types of encryption software. This assurance and commitment shall survive termination of the Agreement. In addition, because the U.S. export control laws currently prohibit nationals of Cuba, Iran, Libya, North Korea and Syria from gaining access to certain Content on the AOL Service, nationals of these countries currently may not legally access the AOL Service at this time.

(d) Benefit of Provisions.

The foregoing provisions of this section 2.6 are for the benefit of AOL Inc. and its independent third-party information providers ("Information Providers"), merchants ("Merchants") and licensors ("Licensors"), and each shall have the right to assert and enforce such provisions directly on their own behalf.

2.7 Third Party Content.

AOL Inc. is a distributor (and not a publisher) of Content supplied by third parties and Members. Accordingly, AOL Inc. has no more editorial control over such Content than does a public library, bookstore, or newsstand. Any opinions, advice, statements, services, offers, or other information or Content expressed or made available by third parties, including Information Providers, Merchants (as defined herein), Members, or any other user of the AOL Service, are those of the respective author(s) or distributor(s) and not of AOL Inc. NEITHER AOL INC. NOR ANY THIRD-PARTY PROVIDER OF INFORMATION GUARANTEES THE ACCURACY, COMPLETENESS, OR USEFULNESS OF ANY CONTENT, NOR ITS MERCHANTABILITY OR FITNESS FOR ANY PARTICULAR PURPOSE. (Refer to Section 5 below for the complete provisions governing limitation of liabilities and disclaimers of warranty.)

In many instances, the Content available through the AOL Service represents the opinions and judgments of the respective Information Provider, Member, or other user not under contract with AOL Inc. AOL Inc. neither endorses nor is responsible for the accuracy or reliability of any opinion, advice or statement made on the AOL Service by anyone other than authorized AOL Inc. employee spokespersons while acting in their official capacities. (Forum leaders and Member Guides are not authorized spokespersons.) Under no circumstances will AOL Inc. be liable for any loss or damage caused by a Member's reliance on information obtained through the AOL Service. It is the responsibility of Member to evaluate the accuracy, completeness or usefulness of any information, opinion, advice or other Content available through the AOL Service. Please seek the advice of professionals, as appropriate, regarding the evaluation of any specific information, opinion, advice, or other Content.

2.8 Retention of Files.

Member is responsible for retention of all files, information data and other materials as may be necessary for reconstruction of any files, information material or messages lost or misprocessed by AOL Inc.

### 3. Third-Party Sales and Services

3.1 Member may order and purchase merchandise or services from other Members and users of the AOL Service, who are not affiliated with AOL Inc. All transactions concerning third-party ("Merchant") goods or services, including, but not limited to, purchase terms, payment terms, warranties, guarantees, maintenance and delivery, are solely between Merchant and Member. AOL Inc. makes no warranties or representations whatsoever with regard to any good or service provided or offered by any Merchant. AOL Inc. shall not be a party to a transaction between Member and Merchant, or be liable for any cost or damage arising either directly or indirectly from any action or inaction of any Merchant.

### 4. AOL Inc.'s Rights

4.1 AOL Inc. may elect to electronically monitor the Public Areas for adherence to its TOS and may disclose any Content, records or electronic communication of any kind (i) to satisfy any law, regulation or authorized governmental request. (ii) if such disclosure is necessary to operate the AOL Service, or (iii) to protect the rights or property of AOL Inc., its Members, or Information Providers or Merchants.

4.2 AOL Inc. reserves the right to prohibit conduct, communication, or Content which it deems in its discretion to be harmful to individual Members, the communities which make up the AOL Service, AOL Inc.'s or other third-party rights, or to violate any applicable law. Notwithstanding the foregoing, neither AOL Inc. nor its Information Providers have the practical ability to restrict conduct, communication or Content which might violate its TOS prior to transmission on the AOL Service, nor can they ensure prompt editing or removal of questionable Content after online posting. Accordingly, neither AOL Inc. nor any Information Provider shall assume liability for any action or inaction with respect to conduct, communication or Content on the AOL Service.

4.3 AOL Inc. will not intentionally monitor or disclose any private electronic communication unless permitted or required by law. AOL Inc. may terminate immediately without notice any Member who misuses or fails to abide by the TOS, including, without limitation, misuse of the software libraries, discussion boards, E-Mail, or conference areas.

4.4 Unless Member elects otherwise by selecting the appropriate "Marketing Preference" choice (Keyword "Marketing Preferences"), AOL Inc. reserves the right to distribute to merchants or third parties certain general Member information, such as Member's name and mailing address. AOL Inc. will not distribute specific Member billing information (i.e. credit card or checking account numbers).

5. **LIMITATION OF LIABILITY AND DISCLAIMER OF WARRANTY**

5.1 MEMBER EXPRESSLY AGREES THAT USE OF THE AOL SERVICE IS AT MEMBER'S SOLE RISK. NEITHER AOL INC., ITS EMPLOYEES, AFFILIATES, AGENTS, THIRD-PARTY INFORMATION PROVIDERS, MERCHANTS, LICENSORS OR THE LIKE, WARRANT THAT THE AOL SERVICE WILL BE UNINTERRUPTED OR ERROR FREE; NOR DO THEY MAKE ANY WARRANTY AS TO THE RESULTS THAT MAY BE OBTAINED FROM THE USE OF THE AOL SERVICE, OR AS TO THE ACCURACY, RELIABILITY OR CONTENT OF ANY INFORMATION, SERVICE, OR MERCHANDISE PROVIDED THROUGH THE AOL SERVICE. NEITHER AOL INC. NOR ANY OF ITS INDEPENDENT NETWORK SERVICE PROVIDERS MAKE ANY REPRESENTATIONS OR WARRANTIES, EITHER EXPRESSED OR IMPLIED, THAT ANY AVAILABLE ACCESS NUMBER WILL BE A LOCAL CALL FROM YOUR AREA CODE AND EXCHANGE.

5.2 THE AOL SERVICE IS PROVIDED ON AN "AS IS," "AS AVAILABLE" BASIS WITHOUT WARRANTIES OF ANY KIND, EITHER EXPRESSED OR IMPLIED, INCLUDING, BUT NOT LIMITED TO, WARRANTIES OF TITLE OR IMPLIED WARRANTIES OF MERCHANTABILITY OR FITNESS FOR A PARTICULAR PURPOSE, OTHER THAN THOSE WARRANTIES WHICH ARE IMPLIED BY AND INCAPABLE OF EXCLUSION, RESTRICTION OR MODIFICATION UNDER THE LAWS APPLICABLE TO THIS AGREEMENT. NO ORAL ADVICE OR WRITTEN INFORMATION GIVEN BY AOL, INC., ITS EMPLOYEES, AGENTS (INCLUDING MEMBER REPRESENTATIVES OR GUIDES), THIRD-PARTY INFORMATION PROVIDERS, MERCHANTS, LICENSORS OR THE LIKE, SHALL CREATE A WARRANTY; NOR SHALL MEMBER RELY ON ANY SUCH INFORMATION OR ADVICE.

5.3 UNDER NO CIRCUMSTANCES, INCLUDING NEGLIGENCE, SHALL AOL INC., OR ANYONE ELSE INVOLVED IN CREATING, PRODUCING

OR DISTRIBUTING THE AOL SERVICE OR THE AOL SOFTWARE, BE LIABLE FOR ANY DIRECT, INDIRECT, INCIDENTAL, SPECIAL OR CONSEQUENTIAL DAMAGES THAT RESULT FROM THE USE OF OR INABILITY TO USE THE AOL SERVICE INCLUDING, BUT NOT LIMITED TO, RELIANCE BY A MEMBER ON ANY INFORMATION OBTAINED ON THE AOL SERVICE; OR THAT RESULT FROM MIS-TAKES, OMISSIONS, INTERRUPTIONS, DELETION OF FILES OR E-MAIL, ERRORS, DEFECTS, VIRUSES, DELAYS IN OPERATION, OR TRANSMISSION, OR ANY FAILURE OF PERFORMANCE, WHETHER OR NOT LIMITED TO ACTS OF GOD, COMMUNICATIONS FAILURE, THEFT, DESTRUCTION OR UNAUTHORIZED ACCESS TO AOL INC.'S RECORDS, PROGRAMS OR SERVICES. MEMBER HEREBY ACKNOWL-EDGES THAT THIS PARAGRAPH 5.3 SHALL APPLY TO ALL CON-TENT, MERCHANDISE OR SERVICES AVAILABLE THROUGH THE AOL SERVICE. BECAUSE SOME STATES DO NOT ALLOW THE EXCLUSION OR LIMITATION OF LIABILITY FOR CONSEQUENTIAL OR INCIDENTAL DAMAGES, IN SUCH STATES AOL'S LIABILITY IS LIMITED TO THE GREATEST EXTENT PERMITTED BY LAW.

5.4 NOTWITHSTANDING THE FOREGOING, IN NO EVENT SHALL THE TOTAL LIABILITY OF AOL INC., OR ITS EMPLOYEES, AFFILIATES, AGENTS, THIRD-PARTY INFORMATION PROVIDERS, MERCHANTS OR LICENSORS, FOR ALL DAMAGES, LOSSES AND CAUSES OF ACTION WHETHER IN CONTRACT, TORT, INCLUDING NEGLIGENCE, OR OTHERWISE, EITHER JOINTLY OR SEVERALLY, EXCEED THE AGGREGATE DOLLAR AMOUNT PAID BY MEMBER TO AOL INC. IN THE TWELVE (12) MONTHS PRIOR TO THE CLAIMED INJURY OR DAMAGE. The foregoing provisions of this Section 5 are for the benefit of AOL Inc., its employees, directors, affiliates, agents, Information Providers, Merchants and Licensors, and each shall have the right to assert and enforce the provisions directly on their behalf.

6. **Software License and Use (omitted from this excerpt)**

7. **Indemnification**

7.1 Upon request of AOL Inc., Member agrees to defend, indemnify and hold harmless AOL Inc. its officers, directors, employees, agents, third party Information Providers, Merchants and Licensees, from any claims and expenses, including reasonable attorney's fees, related to any violation of the TOS by use of Member's Master Account(s), or in connection with the placement or transmission by or through Member of any Content on the AOL Service and its third party Information Providers, Merchants and Members.

8. **Termination**

8.1 Either Member or AOL Inc. may terminate Membership at any time. Member's only right with respect to any dissatisfaction with any (i) TOS term or policy, guideline, or practice of AOL Inc. in operating the AOL Service, (ii)Content available through the AOL Service or change therein, or (iii) change in the amount or type of fees charged in connection with the AOL Service, is to terminate Membership by delivering notice to AOL Inc., effective the day AOL Inc. receives notification of termination or such specified future date as may be acceptable to AOL Inc. In the event that a Member's Master Account is terminated or canceled, any online time credited to Member's Master Account(s) is not convertible to cash or other form of credit.

8.2 AOL Inc. may terminate Membership, or suspend any individual Member's access to all or part of the AOL Service, without notice, for any conduct that AOL Inc. in its sole discretion believes violates the TOS, interferes with another Member's enjoyment of the AOL Service, or is harmful to another Member, third-party Information Provider, Merchant, licensor, service provider or AOL Inc.'s interests.

8.3 Termination of Membership automatically terminates service to all other users or sub-accounts under Member's Master Account. Upon termination of Membership, Member shall have no right to (1) access any stored Content on the AOL Service and any such Content will be forfeited, (2) any user time, game, or other credit(s) and such credit(s) will be forfeited, (3) third-party merchandise or services and AOL, Inc. shall have no responsibility to notify any third-party Merchants, nor for any consequences resulting from lack of notification. Termination or suspension by AOL Inc. automatically terminates or suspends, as the case may be, Member's license to use AOL Software as provided herein. In the event of Termination, Member remains bound by Sections 2, 5, 6, 7, and 9 herein.

9. **Miscellaneous**

9.1 Construction.

In the event that any portion of the TOS is held to be invalid or unenforceable, the invalid or unenforceable portion shall be construed in accordance with applicable law as nearly as possible to reflect the original intentions of the parties, and the remainder of the TOS shall remain in full force and effect. The paragraph headings herein are provided only for reference and shall have no effect on the construction or interpretation of the TOS.

9.2 No Implied Waiver/Modification.

The failure of either party to insist upon or enforce strict performance by the other party of any provision of the TOS shall not be construed as a waiver of any provision or right. Neither the course of conduct between parties nor trade practice shall act to modify any provision of the TOS.

9.3 Applicable Law.

The TOS shall be governed by and construed in accordance with the laws of the Commonwealth of Virginia, except with regard to its conflicts of law rules. Each party irrevocably consents to the exclusive jurisdiction of the courts of the Commonwealth of Virginia and the federal courts situated in the Commonwealth of Virginia in connection with any action arising under the TOS or relating to the AOL Service or AOL Software. Any cause of action of Member or its authorized user(s) with respect to the AOL Service or AOL Software must be commenced within one (1) year after the claim or cause of action arose, or be barred.

9.4 Trademarks.

The "America Online(R) Service" is a registered service mark of AOL Inc. "AOL" is a service mark of AOL Inc. All rights reserved. All other trademarks appearing on the AOL Service are the property of their respective owners.

**Appendix**

## Rules of the Road

A.   These Rules of the Road set forth how America Online, Inc. ("AOL Inc.") will operate the America Online Service ("AOL Service") and how Members may use the AOL Service. The Rules of the Road also explain many practical aspects of using the AOL Service. Please read this document carefully and refer to it as often as necessary. You should also read the Terms of Service ("TOS") Agreement. This document, the TOS Agreement, and the Membership Conditions (which you saw when you first signed on) are all of the applicable AOL Service rules and collectively comprise the contract between AOL Inc. and Members and are referred to as the "Terms of Service" or "TOS." You can view all of the TOS on the AOL Service at any time free of charge in the "Members' Online Support" department located within the "Members Services" area.

B.   We believe that these Terms of Service will enhance AOL Inc.'s efforts to make the AOL Service informative, entertaining and, above all, FUN!! for all our Members. We have tried to explain clearly our Terms of Service, but if any aspect of the TOS is unclear, we welcome your comments. We hope that these Terms of Service will foster an online community where there is both free exchange of ideas and information, and respect for individual and community rights.

## Access

(i)   Equipment.

Most Members will access the AOL Service through a standard residential telephone line, a modem, and a personal computer. (Please remember that when you are connected to the AOL Service, your telephone or other communications equipment, e.g., fax, cannot be operated on the same line at the same time.) There are a variety of personal computers that are capable of accessing and using the AOL Service. For specific technical questions, use the keyword "Techlive." Tech Live is currently open weekdays from 9 a.m. to 2 a.m. (Eastern time) and weekends from 12 p.m. to 1 a.m.

(ii)  Telephone Charges.

You are responsible for all telephone charges incurred in connecting to the AOL Service through the most locally available access number(s) (sometimes referred to as the local access nodes). DEPENDING ON YOUR PARTICULAR LOCATION, THE ACCESS NUMBER IS USUALLY, BUT NOT ALWAYS A LOCAL TELEPHONE CALL. To find additional or closer access numbers use keyword "Access." If you have any questions about which telephone number is best or whether an access number is a local call, please check with your local phone company. Any disputes or problems regarding phone service are strictly between Member and the applicable local phone company and/or long distance service provider.

Please note that AOL Inc. does not maintain the access numbers used to connect to the AOL Service; rather they are owned and operated by independent network service providers. MEMBERS ACCESSING THE AOL SERVICE FROM CANADA WILL BE ASSESSED A SURCHARGE, WHICH IS CURRENTLY TWELVE (12) DOLLARS PER HOUR.

If you cannot currently find an access number that is a local call, check the "New Access Number Updates," which is updated monthly and available in the free Members' Online Support department. (We are continuously expanding the list of local numbers.) You can also call your long-distance telephone company to see if a calling plan is available to allow you to call a long-distance access number for a flat rate, or to purchase blocks of calling time in advance at a discount.

## Your AOL Service Account

(i)  YOU MUST BE AT LEAST EIGHTEEN (18) YEARS OF AGE TO REGISTER FOR THE AOL SERVICE AND BECOME AN AUTHORIZED MEMBER; HOWEVER, A PARENT OR LEGAL GUARDIAN MAY AUTHORIZE A MINOR TO USE HIS/HER ACCOUNT(S) UNDER ADULT SUPERVISION. In that case, the parent or legal guardian recognizes that he/she is fully responsible for the online conduct of such minor, for controlling the minor's access to and use of the AOL Service, and for the consequences of any misuse. The AOL Service offers a "Parental Control" feature that enables the Master Account holder to restrict access to certain areas and features on the AOL Service. Please refer to the Parental Control area in the Members' Online Support department for an explanation of this feature.

(ii)  You are responsible for maintaining the confidentiality of your password. For security purposes, we recommend that you change your password often. (You can do this by entering the "Change Your Personal Password" area in the free Members' Online Support department.) Although the AOL Service offers a feature that allows you to bypass the password protection, please remember that this feature permits anyone who has access to your computer to easily access your account. Use of this password bypass feature is at your own risk. YOU ARE FULLY LIABLE FOR ALL CHARGES UNDER YOUR ACCOUNT AND/OR SUB-ACCOUNT(S), INCLUDING ANY UNAUTHORIZED CHARGES TO YOUR ACCOUNT, UNTIL YOU NOTIFY AOL OF ANY BREACH OF SECURITY. . . .

(iii)  Current rates for using the AOL Service may be obtained by using keyword "billing."

(iv)  AOL reserves the right to distribute to merchants or third parties certain general Member information, such as Member's name and mailing address, unless Member elects otherwise by selecting the appropriate "Marketing Preferences" choice within the "Personal Choices" area on the AOL Service. AOL will not distribute specific billing information (i.e. credit card and checking account numbers).

(v)  AOL encourages you to be creative and have fun with the screen names you choose, but you are also expected to be reasonable and responsible; vulgar or otherwise offensive screen names can offend the sensibilities of many Members, and it is only common courtesy to remember this when you are selecting screen names. You may not use a screen name to impersonate someone, or a name protected by trademark or copyright law. You may use a name of a historical person, but not of another living person. If you are unsure about a screen name, send us a E-Mail using the "Write to Terms of Service Staff" button under keyword "TOS," and select the "Names/Profiles Violations" button. Unfortunately, some Members occasionally select vulgar or otherwise offensive screen names as a joke, or just a momentary lapse of good judgment. AOL Inc. reserves the right to delete any such screen name, or to request deletion.

## Online Conduct

Please refer to Section 2.5 of the Terms of Service Agreement for AOL Inc's policy on impermissible types of online conduct. Below are some common violations of the Terms of Service. This list is not exhaustive. AOL Inc. reserves the right, but does not assume the responsibility, to restrict communication which AOL Inc. deems in its discretion to be harmful to individual Members, damaging to the communities which make up the AOL Service, or in violation of AOL Inc.'s or any third-party rights. Please be aware, however, that communication over the AOL Service often occurs in real-time, or is posted on one of the AOL Service's thousands of message boards or libraries, and AOL Inc. cannot, and does not intend to, screen communication in advance.

If you witness chat in a public chat room that violates AOL's Terms of Service, you may contact an AOL Service Guide by using the keyword "Guide Pager." You may also contact AOL's Terms of Service Staff about any violation by using the "Write to the Terms of Service Staff" icon located in the Terms of Service area of the Member's Online Support department.

## Offensive Communication

The AOL Service is a community-oriented service composed of many different communities of people. Our goal is to provide an interesting, stimulating and fun place for all Members. Using vulgar, abusive or hateful language undermines this goal and is not allowed. Please use your best judgment and be respectful of other Members. Remember, there are children online.

If you use vulgar, or abusive language online, even if masked by symbols or other characters, you may either receive an "on-screen-warning" by a Guide or Room Host, or in extreme cases be terminated immediately.

A warning indicates that your language is not in compliance with AOL Inc.'s Rules.

Should you receive such a warning, take the time to read the TOS Agreement again and these Rules of the Road posted in the free Members' Online Support department.

## Harassment

When a Member targets another specifically to cause him/her distress, embarrassment, unwanted attention, or other discomfort, this is harassment.

AOL Inc. does not condone harassment in any form and may suspend or terminate the accounts of any Member who harasses others.

You may have a disagreement with someone's point of view—we encourage lively discussion in our chat rooms and message boards—but personal attacks, or attacks based on a person's race, national origin, ethnicity, religion, gender, sexual orientation or other such affiliation, are prohibited.

If you have a disagreement with someone's point of view, address the subject, not the person.

## Graphic Files

AOL Inc. prohibits the transfer or posting on the AOL Service of sexually explicit images or other content deemed offensive by AOL Inc.

## Scrolling

"Scrolling" means repeatedly causing the screen to roll faster than Members are able to type to it. It is caused by a user entering a set of random characters or by repeatedly entering a carriage return or any such action to a similar disruptive effect. Scrolling is an expressly prohibited form of disruption.

## Room Disruption

This includes purposefully interfering with the normal flow of dialogue in a chat room. Room disruption may occur by repeatedly interrupting conversation between Members, or by acting in such a way as to antagonize, harass or create hostility in a chat room.

## The 3 R's of E-Mail

## Impersonation

This can involve the portrayal of an account in an official capacity, such as AOL Inc. staff or an information provider, authorized Guide or Host, or communication under a false name or a name that you are not authorized to use.

Members must avoid the portrayal of AOL personnel or other persons in all forms of online communication, including, but not limited to, screen names, member profiles, chat dialogue and message postings.

## Polling

Polling is a form of Room disruption whereas a member questions the room at large for an immediate and specific answer resulting in a massive scroll of responses.

> i.e.     If you like XXXXXXX press XXXXX now.
> If you want to XXXXXXX press XXXXX now.

## Chain Letters and Pyramid Schemes

Transmission of chain letters and pyramid schemes of any kind is not allowed on the AOL Service. This material places an unnecessary load on our mail system and is considered a nuisance by many Members.

Certain chain letters and pyramid schemes are illegal.

Letters or messages that offer a product or service based on the structure of a chain letter are also of questionable legality. At minimum, they are a waste of resources and are not permitted on the AOL Service.

## Advertising and Solicitation

You may not use the AOL Service to send unsolicited advertising, promotional material, or other forms of solicitation to other Members except in those specified areas that are designated for such a purpose (e.g., the classified area).

## *Third-Party Content and Information*

Because AOL Inc. encourages open and candid communication, it cannot determine in advance the accuracy of Content transmitted on the AOL Service. AOL is not responsible for screening, policing, editing, or monitoring such Content. If notified of allegedly infringing, defamatory, damaging, illegal or offensive Content, AOL Inc., may investigate the allegation and determine in good faith and in its sole discretion whether to remove or request the removal of such Content from the AOL Service. AOL Inc. shall be held harmless from any performance or non-performance by AOL Inc. of such activities, as long as it has acted in good faith.

Please use your best judgment in evaluating all information contained or opinions expressed on the AOL Service. You should be at least as careful in your evaluation of such information and opinions on the AOL Service as you are in everyday life. It is AOL Inc.'s policy not to endorse, oppose, or edit any opinion expressed by a Member or information or material provided by an independent contractor.

Independent contractors who supply information or content to the AOL Service ("Information Provider") endeavor to make it accurate and reliable, but do not guarantee or warrant as so. In some instances, the information provided may represent opinion and judgment and/or may have been supplied by a Member not in any way under a contract with AOL Inc.

## Internet Access and Conduct

The AOL Service features comprehensive access to the Internet. When using the Internet and all of its components, Members must conduct themselves responsibly according to the Internet's own particular code of conduct. Participating successfully on the Internet is really a matter of common sense. Although AOL Inc. does not control the Internet, your conduct on the Internet when using your AOL account is subject to the Terms of Service. Because AOL Inc. wants to be a good Internet citizen, it prohibits Members from engaging in certain conduct on the Internet through or by means of the AOL Service including the following:

(i) Chain Letters. Chain letters are prohibited on the AOL Service and are inappropriate on the Internet. Posting a chain letter to an Internet newsgroup (or via E-Mail on the Internet) may result in your AOL Service account being terminated.

(ii) Commercial Communication. The vast majority of newsgroups and mailing lists on the Internet are not commercial in nature and participants in such groups may object strongly to commercial postings, solicitations, or advertisements.

(iii) Other Inappropriate Posts. Each newsgroup and mailing list on the Internet focuses on a particular set of topics and posts not related to these topics are not welcomed by the participants. We suggest that all AOL Service Members become familiar with the guidelines, themes, and culture of the specific newsgroups and mailing list in which they wish to participate. Posting patently inappropriate material on the Internet may result in suspension or termination of your AOL Service account.

(iv) Copyrighted and Proprietary Materials. Transmitting to the Internet copyrighted or other proprietary materials of any kind without the express permission of the right holder is prohibited and will result in termination of your Membership and possible civil and/or criminal liability.

Additionally, AOL Inc. does not control the Internet and therefore use of the Internet is at Member's own risk. Members should exercise their discretion and supervision when allowing any minors under their Master Account to access the Internet.

## Purchasing Products and Services through the AOL Service

Please remember that AOL Inc. does not endorse, warrant, or guarantee any product or service offered through the AOL Service and will not be a party to any transaction between you and third-party providers of products or services. As with the purchase of a product or service through any medium or in any environment, you should use your best judgment and exercise caution where appropriate. Blind opportunity ads and "get rich quick" schemes should be approached with ample skepticism. The AOL Service cannot mediate disputes and cannot assume responsibility for any outcome. Be careful, be smart, have fun!

## Public and Private Communication

The AOL Service offers Members the capability to communicate in Public Areas generally accessible to other Members or to communicate privately with another Member. Public Areas are those features that are generally accessible to other Members, such as, but not limited to, chat rooms, online forums, and message boards. Private Communication is electronic correspondence sent or received by you to particular individuals. AOL Inc. will maintain the AOL Service Public Areas as an open forum for discussion of a wide range of issues and expression of diverse viewpoints. AOL Inc. will administer standards of online conduct according to its TOS for the enjoyment of all its Members. While we will endeavor to monitor the Public Areas to ensure that online standards are being maintained, AOL Inc. has neither the practical capability, nor does it intend, to act in the role of "Big Brother" by screening public communication in advance.

It is AOL Inc.'s policy to respect the privacy of personal electronic communication. AOL Inc. will not intentionally inspect the contents of an electronic message ("E-Mail" or "Instant Message") sent by one Member to another individual, monitor discussions in private rooms, or disclose the contents of any personal electronic communication to an unauthorized third party, except as required or permitted to do so by law. AOL Inc. reserves the right to cooperate fully with local, state, or federal officials in any investigation relating to any Content, including private electronic communication, transmitted on the AOL Service or the unlawful activities of any Member.

AOL Inc. reserves the right to remove any Content that it deems in its sole discretion to be a violation of its Terms of Service. AOL Inc. may terminate immediately any Member who misuses or fails to abide by its Terms of Service.

AOL, Inc.'s current general practice is that (i) E-Mail is retained on the AOL Service for five (5) days after the date it is read and then permanently deleted and (ii) unread E-Mail is kept on the AOL Service for approximately thirty (30) days; however, AOL Inc. makes no warranties of any kind with respect to its E-Mail service and is not responsible for any message which may be misprocessed by AOL Inc.

*Note:* AOL's Terms of Service is reprinted with permission from AOL Corporate Communications, April 10, 1995. A couple of omissions (items not applicable to this book) and formatting changes (bolding, italics, and indentations) have been made to the original text obtained online.

# Suggested
# Sources

# Books and Other Sources

Angell, David and Brent Heslop, *The Elements of E-mail Style*, Reading, Massachusetts: Addison-Wesley Publishing Company, 1994.

Baker, Richard H. *Network Security: How to Plan for It and Achieve It,* New York: McGraw-Hill, 1995.

Cavazos, Edward A. and Gavino Morin, *Cyberspace and the Law,* Cambridge: The MIT Press, 1994.

Currid, Cheryl. *Electronic Invasion: Brave New World of Business Communications,* New York: Brady Publishing, 1993.

"Guidelines for Company Policies On Employee Privacy in the Electronic Workplace," Center for Information Technology and Law, College of Business Administration-College of Law, University of Cincinnati, Cincinnati, OH 45221-0387

Hartman, Diane B. and Karen S. Nantz. "Summary of Electronic Messaging Survey: CPS® Seminar, June 1994.

Hartman, Diane B. and Karen S. Nantz. "E-Mail Audit Form A," 1995.

Hartman, Diane B. and Karen S. Nantz. "E-Mail Audit Form B," 1995.

Johnson, David R. and John Podesta, "Access to and Use and Disclosure of Electronic Mail on Company Computer Systems: A Tool Kit for Formulating Your Company's Policy," Baltimore, Maryland: Electronic Messaging Association, 1990.

Johnson, David R. and John Podesta, "Formulating An Electronic Mail Privacy Policy," A non-technical summary of the White Paper Access to and Use and Disclosure of Electronic Mail on Company Computer Systems: A Tool Kit for Formulating Your Company's Policy, Electronic Messaging Association, 1990.

Negroponte, Nicholas. *Being Digital,* New York: Alfred A. Knopf, 1995.

Podesta, John and Michael Sher. *Protecting Electronic Messaging: A Guide to the Electronic Communications Privacy Act of 1986.* Arlington, Virginia: The Electronic Messaging Association, 1990.

Rifkin, Jeremy, *The End of Work,* New York: GP Putnam's Sons, 1995.

Rose, Lance. *Netlaw,* New York: Osborne-McGraw Hill, 1995.

Stoll, Clifford. *Silicon Snake Oil,* New York: Doubleday, 1995.

Wright, Benjamin. *The Law of Electronic Commerce,* Boston: Little, Brown and Company, 1991.

# Associations

Electronic Frontier Foundation
1001 G Street. NW, Suite 950 E
Washington, DC 20001, USA
202/234-5400
fax: 292/393-5509
e-mail: info@eff.org or ask@eff.org

Electronic Messaging Association
PO Box 79284
Baltimore, MD 21279-0284
703/524-5550
fax: 703/524-5558
e-mail: info@ema.org

Electronic Privacy Information Center
666 Pennsylvania Avenue SE, Suite 301
Washington, DC 20003
202/547-5482
e-mail: epic@cpsr.org

Computer Professionals for Social Responsibility (CPSR)
PO Box 717
Palo Alto, CA 94302 USA
415/322-3778
fax: 415/322-3798
cpsr@csli.standford.edu

**Suggested Sources**

## Conferences

Computers, Freedom and Privacy (CFP). Held in March each year at a selected location. To subscribe to the CPSR mailing list, e-mail: listserv@cpsr.org

Electronic Messaging Association Annual Conference and Exposition held in the spring each year and Messaging Solutions Summit held in the fall each year. For more information, contact the Electronic Messaging Association by phone (703/524-5550), by fax (703/524-5558), or by e-mail (Internet: info@ema.org•X.400:S=info; O=ema; A=mci; C=us•World Wide Web: http://www.ema.org) .

# Glossary

| | |
|---|---|
| Bulletin board system (BBS) | An electronic message board to which people may post e-mail messages. |
| Clipper chip | U.S. government's proposed encryption method to allow government authorities to hold keys to encrypted communications. |
| Common carrier status | Public service that indiscriminately transfers people, property and information. |
| Company record | Information vital to an organization's operation. |
| Copyright Act | Federal law that protects owners against others distributing, copying, modifying, transmitting or making public an original work that is fixed in a tangible medium. It does not extend to any idea, procedure, process, system, method of operation, concept, principle or discovery. |
| Cyberspace | A term coined by William Gibson in his fantasy novel, *Neuromancer,* to describe the world of computers and the society that gathers around them. |
| Defamation | Harm caused by false or damaging statements published to an audience other than just the plaintiff. |
| libel | written defamatory statements |
| slander | spoken defamatory statements |
| Digitized images | Graphic images converted to a digital format. |
| E-cash | Electronic money exchanged outside established networks of banks, checks and paper regulated by the Federal Reserve. |

| | |
|---|---|
| E-chat | Real-time online electronic conversations. |
| ECPA | Electronic Communications Privacy Act is a federal law that prohibits the interception or disclosure of private communications sent over public lines. |
| Electronic mail (e-mail) | Electronic communication of text, data, image or voice messages between a sender and designated recipients by systems utilizing telecommunication links. |
| E-mail header | First part of an e-mail message containing address information: To, Cc, Subject and Attachment lines of a message. |
| E-Mail audit | A questionnaire or survey completed by employees (both users and nonusers) to provide open, honest and accurate information about how users perceive and use e-mail. |
| E-mail policy | A clear statement of guidelines and boundaries for what a provider and user can do using e-mail. A lenient policy attempts to set general e-mail boundaries but does not attempt to restrict or monitor user messages. A restrictive policy tends to curtail employee personal e-mail messages and focuses on e-mail as a business tool. A restrictive policy also specifies how employees will be punished if e-mail guidelines are not followed. |
| Emoticons and smileys | Visual shorthand substituting for missing nonverbal clues to meaning. Smileys use punctuation marks to resemble facial expressions. |
| Encryption | Scrambling or coding information to ensure privacy. |

| | |
|---|---|
| **European Community** | The European Community (EC) will establish unilateral policies for the transfer of information among the 12 member countries. |
| **Fair use** | The fair use section of the copyright law allows copyrighted works to be reproduced for the following purposes: criticism, comment, news reporting, teaching (including multiple copies for classroom use), scholarship and research. |
| **FAQs** | Frequently asked questions associated with many user groups, especially helpful to newcomers. |
| **Filter** | Utility program that allows a computer user to screen and prioritize incoming messages according to a set of criteria: keywords, names, message topics. |
| **Firewalls** | Barriers between internal and external networks that screen incoming messages and allow only authorized users access to the internal system. |
| **First Amendment** | Guarantees protection against government oppression but does not apply to private acts. |
| **Flame** | A flame attacks another user or a group of users. Contains derogatory or embarrassing information that may include insensitive, profane or obscene language and may be argumentative. In response, others may attack the original sender (the flamer) and spark a flame war. |
| **Fourth Amendment** | Protects citizens from unreasonable governmental searches and seizures. |
| **Gateway** | A special-purpose dedicated computer that attaches to two or more networks and |

routes messages from one network to the other.

Hacker

Usually a skilled programmer who tries to gain unauthorized access to computer systems.

Hole in WWW

A "hole" in the World Wide Web allows intruders into an area frequented by businesses for the purpose of extracting information for unauthorized use.

Home Page

Hyperlinked document with embedded commands that allow the user to move from one document to another.

Hypertext

Highly interconnected narrative or linked information. By clicking on a word or phrase, a user can go directly to related files.

Indecent material

Sexual material not suited for minors.

Information Highway

Term usually referring to the Internet and its interconnected networks.

Interactive marketing

Senders and receivers can exchange information for business purposes.

Internet

A system of wide area networks supported by universities, research centers and government agencies that allows international transmission of data.

Jargon

Words and phrases used by a limited audience.

Local area network (LAN)

A computer network that links computers at a single site, such as a department or building. Local area networks allow users to share hardware, software and data and to send and receive data and graphics files.

| | |
|---|---|
| **Lurking** | Anonymously reading electronic postings without responding. |
| **Mail address** | A mail address is the unique electronic location of your e-mail files. A mail address usually consists of two parts: the name of the host computer where your e-mail system is located and your specific mailing address. For example: jsmith@abccorp.com might be the mailing address for John Smith at ABC Corporation. |
| **Message channel** | Medium used to communicate: fax, voice, face-to-face, e-mail, surface mail, video conferencing, teleconferencing, etc. |
| **Monitoring** | The checking of online messages by organizations and their system administrators. |
| **Mosaic** | Software that allows the user to access hypermedia resources through a graphical user interface, such as Windows. |
| **Multimedia** | A term used to refer to media for communicating information: text, audio, video, graphics. |
| **Newsgroup** | A newsgroup is a place within a LAN or WAN where discussions on a particular topic take place. Users send and receive articles from the newsgroup. The common set of newsgroups is Usenet that allows newsgroups on the Internet. |
| **Netiquette** | A pun on "etiquette"; proper behavior in sending and receiving electronic messages. |
| **Newbies** | New users who ask elementary questions and who fail to observe the conventions followed by online veterans. |

| | |
|---|---|
| **Obscene material** | Sexual material that offends an average person according to a selected community standard, is considered patently offensive and, as a whole based on a national standard, is obscene. |
| **Online services** | Commercial electronic messaging subscriber services such as America Online, Compu-Serve and Prodigy. |
| **Password sniffers** | Hidden computer programs that record and store logons and passwords. |
| **Previewing** | Checking an electronic mail header to determine which messages to read. |
| **Public domain** | Information dedicated by the owner to be free of copyright restrictions; however, formatting, sequencing, comments and even summaries may remain copyrighted. |
| **Real-time chat** | Chat that takes place without minimal delays. |
| **Remailer** | A person who helps ship data around the world in complete anonymity. |
| **Server** | A computer that shares its resources such as printers and files with other computers on the network. |
| **Snail mail** | Traditional mail (surface mail) sent through the U.S. Post Office |
| **Spoofing** | A software program that gains "root" access usually available only to a system operator; it acts as a "back door" to the system and its valuable information. |
| **Surfing** | Browsing the Internet or any other wide area network. |

| | |
|---|---|
| **System administrator or operator (Sysop)** | Electronic-system operators responsible for maintaining and securing the network. Also referred to as the e-mail overseer, gate-keeper and referee. |
| **Thread** | A central theme or message topic. |
| **Usenet** | A collection of more than 5,000 special-interest public forums on the Internet. |
| **User's agreement or contract** | An agreement that outlines the organization's and the user's expectations and establishes guidelines for proper use and security of the system. |
| **Wide area network (WAN)** | A computer network that links computers together in a wide geographical area. A WAN functions the same as a LAN but allows wide distribution of data and graphics files. |
| **Warrant** | A legal document required by authorities before they can enter and seize equipment or information. |
| **Work in progress** | Preliminary thoughts and ideas that may not reflect an organization's official record. |
| **Work for hire** | Refers to work created within the scope of employment; gives the employer ownership to that work. |
| **World Wide Web (WWW)** | System for organizing information on the Internet using hypertext links. By clicking on a highlighted word or phrase, a user can move from one web site to another. |

# References

## Introduction

1. Rothfeder, Jeffrey. "E-mail snooping; electronic mail privacy issues," *Corporate Computing,* vol. 1 no. 3, Sept. 1992, p. 168.

## Section I

1. "Messaging," *PC Magazine,* April 25, 1995, p. 108.

2. "No failure to communicate," *Datamation,* April 15, 1995, p. 16.

3. Berger, Alan and Sid Bratkovich, "Computer hardware and software news summary," *Hi-Tech Notes,* vol. 13 no. 2, Jan. 15, 1995.

4. Case, Steve. "A letter from Case," America Online, July 1, 1995.

5. Berger and Bratkovich, "Computer hardware and software news summary," *Hi-Tech Notes,* vol. 13 no. 1, Jan. 1, 1995.

6. Rifkin, Jeremy. *The End of Work.* New York: GP Putnam's Sons, 1995.

7. Stoll, Clifford. *Silicon Snake Oil.* New York: Doubleday, 1995, pp. 17, 30.

8. "Caught up in the net," *Beyond Computing,* June 1995, p. 10.

9. Zachary, G. Pascal. "It's a mail thing: electronic messaging gets a rating—ex," *Wall Street Journal,* June 24, 1994, A1.

10. Coffee, Peter. "E-mail is ready, but are companies primed?" *PCWeek,* Oct. 18, 1993, vol. 10 no. 41, p. 38.

11. "Managing unruly desktop," *Wall Street Journal,* Feb. 16, 1995, A1.

## Section II

1. Cosentino, Victor J. "Virtual legality: once online, some people totally disregard legally and socially acceptable behavior," *Byte,* March 1994, vol. 19 no. 3, p. 278.

2. Podesta, John and Michael Sher. *Protecting electronic messaging: A guide to the Electronic Communications Act of 1986.* The Electronic Messaging Association, 1990, p. x, xi.

3. Stahl, Stephanie. "Dangerous e-mail," *Information Week,* Sept. 12, 1994, p. 13.

## The 3 R's of E-Mail

4. Ibid.

5. Cavazos, Edward A. and Gavino Morin. *Cyberspace and the Law.* Cambridge, Mass.: The MIT Press, 1994, pp. 26, 124.

6. Van Kirk, Doug. "IS managers balance privacy rights and risks," *InfoWorld,* Nov. 29, 1993, vol. 15 no. 48, p. 65(1).

7. Rose, Lance. *Netlaw: Your Rights in the Online World.* New York: Osborne McGraw-Hill, 1995, pp. 161-162.

8. Cavazos and Morin, p. 60.

9. Op. cit., p. 74.

10. Op cit., pp., 82–83.

11. Quittner, Joshua. "Vice raid on the net," Time Inc., America Online, March 29, 1995.

12. Pearl, Daniel. "Government tackles a surge of smut on the Internet," *Wall Street Journal,* Feb. 8, 1995, B1.

13. Maskowitz, Robert. "Seven foolproof tips for computer security," *Investors Business Daily,* May 2, 1995.

14. Stets, Dan (*The Philadelphia Inquirer*). *The Salt Lake Tribune,* Salt Lake City, Utah, Jan. 22, 1995, pp. F4, F6.

15. Quittner, Joshua. "Cracks in the net," Time Inc., America Online, Feb. 24, 1995.

16. Reichard, Kevin. "Will your business be safe?" *PC Magazine,* May 16, 1995, vol. 14, no. 9, p. 218 [1].

17. "Warding off the cyberspace invaders," *Business Week,* March 13, 1995.

18. "Management's responsibility to preserve and protect business information," *Managing Office Technology,* Dec. 1993, pp. 19–22.

19. Maskowitz, Robert. "Seven foolproof tips for computer security," *Investors' Business Daily,* May 2, 1995.

20. "Management's responsibility. . . ," p. 22.

21. See Stahl.

22. "E-mail task force pushes OMB for a model government policy," *Government Computer News,* Oct. 3, 1994, vol. 13 no. 22, pp. 1–2.

**References**

23. Du Rea, Mary V. and J. Michael Pemberton. "Electronic mail and electronic data interchange: challenges to records management," *Records Management Quarterly,* Oct. 1994, p. 10.

24. Castro, Janice. "Just click to buy," Special Issue: Welcome to Cyberspace, *Time,* Spring 1995, p. 8–9.

25. Ziegler, Bart. "In cyberspace the Web delivers junk mail," *Wall Street Journal,* June 13, 1995, B1.

26. "The Internet: How it will change the way you do business," *Business Week,* Nov. 14, 1995, p. 80.

27. Castro, op. cit., p. 75.

28. Lewis, Peter H. "Pizza via Internet—but isn't the phone easier?" Times News Service, America Online, April 7, 1995.

29. Holland, Kelley, and Amy Cortese. "The future of money, E-cash could transform the world's financial life" *Business Week,* June 12, 1995.

30. Ibid.

31. "What's the color of cybermoney?" Special Report, *Business Week,* Feb. 27, 1995.

32. Holland and Cortese.

33. Cortese, Amy (editor). "A more secure future for cybershoppers?" *Business Week,* April 24, 1995.

## Section III

1. Young, Lawrence T. and Gordon A. Christenson. *Guidelines for Company Policies on Employee Privacy in the Electronic Workplace: A Report on Sample Policies and Analyses.* The Center for Information Technology and the Law, University of Cincinnati, Cincinnati, Ohio.

2. "Goofing off at work: PC games, e-mail chat put a dent into productivity," *PC Today,* vol. 9 no. 3, March, 1995, pp. 16–19.

3. Van Kirk, Doug, "As Managers Balance Privacy and Risks," *Infoworld,* vol. 15, No. 48, p. 62

4. Casarez, Nicole B. "Electronic mail and employee relations: why privacy must be considered," *Public Relations Quarterly,* vol. 37, Summer, 1992, p. 39.

5. Rothfeder, op. cit.

6. Sharp Paine, Lynn and Albert Choy. "Note on e-mail and privacy: U.S. law and organization policies," Harvard Business School, 1992, pp. 7–8.

7. Rothfeder, op. cit.

8. See Young and Christenson.

9. Coates, James. "Computer privacy? It's not a given," *Chicago Tribune,* Sunday, May 23, 1993.

10. Rothfeder, op. cit.

11. Van Kirk, op. cit., p. 65.

12. Annual Conference and Exposition of the Electronic Messaging Association, May 1995. *Conference Proceedings, Volume II.* New Orleans, Louisiana, pp. 422–423.

13. Kingston, Jeffrey S. and Gregory L. Lippetz. *The Business Journal,* vol. 10 no. 42, p. 21.

14. Podeseta and Sher, op. cit.

15. Ibid., p.41.

16. Cahoon, Tim. "Playing peek-a-boo with e-mail," *HP Professional,* vol. 8 no. 3, March 1994, p. 56.

17. Schrage, Michael. "First Amendment to answer call of telecom oversight," *Los Angeles Times,* Sept. 29, 1994, vol. 113, p. D 1.

18. Swartz, Jon. "Prodigy named in $100 million libel suit," *MacWeek,* vol. 8 no. 46, Nov. 28, 1994, p. 24.

19. Phone interview with James Barresi, attorney-at-law, Cincinnati, Ohio, June 20, 1995.

20. Bairstow, Jeffrey. "Who reads your electronic mail? Issues of Electronic Mail Security," *Electronic Business,* vol. 16 no. 11, June 11, 1990, p. 92.

21. Mace, Scott. "Campaign puts focus on ethics in computing," *Infoworld,* vol. 16 no. 27, July 4, 1994, p. 17.

22. Power, Kevin. "E-mail on every desk by 1997: White House taskforce endorses X.400 and public gateways," *Government Computer News,* vol. 13, No. 8, April 18, 1994, p. 1.

**References**

23. Smith, Laura B. "Electronic monitoring raises legal and societal questions," *PCWeek,* vol. 10 no. 25, June 28, 1993, p. 204.

24. D'Amico, Marie. "The Copyright Act faces down the Net," *Digital Media,* vol. 4 no. 3, Aug. 8, 1994, p. 20.

25. Coates, op. cit.

26. Brown, Bob. "E-mail users voice concern about pending legislation," *Network World,* vol. 10 no. 34, Aug. 23, 1993,p. 6.

27. Alert: S314 Online "Decency Act: threatens all online providers," EFFector Online, vol. 8 no. 1, Feb. 10, 1995.

28. Peterson, Steven. "Cleansing the channels: censorship in cyberspace," ICS Electrozine, Western State College, Gunnison, Colorado, April 19, 1995, p. 4.

29. Resnick, Rosalind. "As personal computers proliferate, the technology raises new civil liberties issues that test the bounds of existing laws," *The National Law Journal,* Sept. 16, 1991.

30. Wright, Benjamin. *The Law of Electronic Commerce.* Boston: Little, Brown, and Co., 1991.

31. Lewis, Peter H. "Persistent e-mail: electronic stalking or innocent courtship?" *New York Times,* vol. 143, p. Bll, Sept. 16,1994.

32. Lewis, Tamar. "Dispute over computer messages: free speech or sexual harassment?" *New York Times,* vol. 144, p. A1, Sept. 22, 1994. (Please note that in footnote 31, the year 1994 of the *NYT* was volume 143; here it is vol. 144. See ms pages 120, 121.)

33. Swartz, op. cit.

34. Newsbytes, Newswatch Forum, The Internet.

35. Schwartz, Anthony. 'E-mail privacy? Not on the job!" *Computer Shopper,* vol. 13 no. 8, p. 623.

36. Ibid.

37. Kingston and Lippetz. 'How private is employee use of e-mail?" *Communication News,* vol. 30 no. 10, Oct. 1993, p. 22.

38. Cooper III, Frederick. "Copyright in cyberspace," *Computer Reseller News,* no. 599, Oct. 10, 1994, p. 97.

39. Braithwaite, Nick. "Why bulletin boards are a libel minefield," *Computer Weekly*, May 12, 1994, p. 28.

40. Green, Robert. "E-mail snooping: believe only half of what you read," *Government Computer News*, vol. 12 no. 23, Oct. 25, 1993, p. 52.

41. Rosenoer, Jonathan. "Photocopy Unlawful," Cyberlaw and CyberLex, America Online, January 1995.

42. Sandberg, Jared. "Newsletter faces libel suit for flaming on the Internet," *The Wall Street Journal*, April 22, 1994, p. B1.

43. Currid, Cheryl. *Electronic Invasion: Brave New World of Business Communications*. New York: Brady Publishing, 1993, p. 119.

## Section IV

1. Associated Press. "Users, activists fight bid to limit Internet access," *Deseret News*, Salt Lake City, Utah, March 6–7, 1995.

2. Mission Statement of the Electronic Frontier Foundation (EEF), Electronic Frontier Forum, Washington, D.C., America Online, Feb. 6, 1995.

3. Hilton, Don. "E-mail unites a campus," *Managing Office Technology*, Dec. 1994, pp. 40–41.

4. Associated Press. "Access Internet, send fax, play games at 30,000 feet," *Deseret News*, Salt Lake City, Utah, March 19, 1995, p. M1.

5. Jackson, James O. "It's a wired, wired world," Welcome to Cyberspace, *Time*, Spring 1995, pp. 80–81.

6. Aiyer Ghosh, Rishab. "Freedom on the Net in India," America Online, Feb. 2, 1992.

7. Dennis, Sylvia. "German government worried about data privacy legislation," America Online, Dec. 2, 1994.

8. Quittner, Joshua. "Unmakes on the Net," Time, Inc., America Online, Feb. 26, 1995.